The Abingdon
Preaching
Annual

2017

**Planning Sermons and Services
for Fifty-Two Sundays**

Scott Hoezee, General Editor

Abingdon Press

Nashville

THE ABINGDON PREACHING ANNUAL 2017:
PLANNING SERMONS AND SERVICES FOR FIFTY-TWO SUNDAYS

Library of Congress Cataloging-in-Publication Data has been requested.

ISBN: 978-1-5018-1514-0

Scripture unless otherwise noted is from the Common English Bible. Copyright © 2011 by the Common English Bible. All rights reserved. Used by permission. www.CommonEnglishBible.com.

Scripture quotations marked NRSV are from the New Revised Standard Version of the Bible, copyright 1989, Division of Christian Education of the National Council of the Churches of Christ in the United States of America. Used by permission. All rights reserved.

Scripture quotations marked *The Message* are from THE MESSAGE. Copyright © by Eugene H. Peterson 1993, 1994, 1995, 1996, 2000, 2001, 2002. Used by permission of NavPress Publishing Group.

The text on pp. 181–83 is from *The Sermon without End: A Conversational Approach to Preaching* by Ronald Allen and O. Wesley Allen Jr. (2015). Copyright © 2015 by Abingdon Press. Used by permission. All rights reserved.

The text on pp. 178–80 is from *Actuality: Real Life Stories for Sermons That Matter* by Scott Hoezee (2014). Copyright © 2014 by Abingdon Press. Used by permission. All rights reserved.

The text on pp. 175–77 is from *Preaching in Pictures: Using Images for Sermons That Connect* by Peter Jonker (2015). Copyright © 2015 by Abingdon Press. Used by permission. All rights reserved.

16 17 18 19 20 21 22 23 24 25—10 9 8 7 6 5 4 3 2 1
MANUFACTURED IN THE UNITED STATES OF AMERICA

Contents

Contents

ESSAYS FOR SKILL-BUILDING

FULL SERMON TEXTS

Introduction

Call it "job security" if you wish, but for preachers there is one inescapable reality: every week has a Sunday. Here and there across any given year there are also weeks with the equivalent of an extra Sunday thrown into the mix in the form of Epiphany, Maundy Thursday and Good Friday, Ascension Day, Christmas. The pace is relentless as is the need for ongoing fresh output of sermons from God's word. After graduating from seminary, I spent the next fifteen years serving as a pastor at two different congregations, both of which had a morning and an evening worship service. A typical calendar year saw me writing between seventy-five to eighty-five new sermons.

If there is one thing that I learned very quickly, it was that without fresh input— a lot of it on an ongoing basis—there was no chance for any fresh homiletical output. For the past eleven years as director of Calvin Theological Seminary's Center for Excellence in Preaching, I have been seeking to provide my fellow preachers with just such fresh input on a weekly basis as well as through continuing education seminars. Now I am pleased to serve as general editor for this volume that seeks to give preachers that needed "jump start" to get rolling on yet another sermon or two on any given week. In this volume you will find energizing ideas and insights from some fellow preachers with the hope that something will spark a novel way to view a given text or present just enough of a new slant on a familiar text as to make that text seem new after all.

We have also provided some sample litanies, prayers, and other liturgical resources to make the weekly task of cobbling together worship services a bit easier even as these resources also go along with the preaching themes presented on lectionary texts. Through it all it is my sincere hope that a task that drains so much out of the preacher might be made a little easier (even as the preacher might get a bit reinvigorated) by receiving a little jolt of new insights and fresh approaches to these texts— texts through which God sends the Good News to the world. Through this I hope that sermons in churches everywhere can shine with all the vibrancy and urgency and beauty that God's word so richly deserves.

—*Scott Hoezee, General Editor*

January 6, 2017
Epiphany

Isaiah 60:1-6; Psalm 72:1-7, 10-14; Ephesians 3:1-12; Matthew 2:1-12

Gathering Prayer

Holy and Sacred One, on this day of anticipation and renewal, we come to you both waiting and wanting. We are hoping and anticipating. We are hungry and weary. We are individuals and a diverse community. Draw us near to you, O God. Remind us of your presence so that we may remember who we are created to be. Amen.

Preaching Theme

Epiphany is commonly referenced as the *aha moment*. An aha moment might remind a person of old cartoons when the character finally figures out how to solve a problem and a light bulb flashes above his or her head. When the wise men came to bring gifts to the Christ child, their gifts showed the world that Jesus came to the world as both Lord and Savior. This week we have an aha moment! This baby is a king! We especially remember that it was the gifts of the wise men that first proclaimed Jesus's rightful glory.

We don't really know how many wise men there were in the year that Jesus was born; tradition says that there were three. They are often remembered as kings— maybe because they brought such royal gifts. Some remember them as astrologers— because they were following a star. They might remind some of the three mysterious guests who visited Abraham.

Sometime around the year 500, a legend arose that they were named Gaspar, Melchior, and Balthasar. For some, we remember their arrival by placing figures of them at the manger during Christmas pageants. Many scholars believe they visited the holy family when Jesus was a toddler. There was a rumor in the eighth century that they were not from the east, as the Gospels state, but that they were from Ireland. Some modern churches in India believe that the magi (or magicians) came from India. Christian tradition in China claims they were Chinese.

Whichever tradition we draw from, we really only know one thing for certain: they were foreigners who traveled from far away to proclaim the miracle of the Christ child.

Secondary Preaching Themes

The texts from Ephesians 3 and Isaiah 60 remind us that our calling is both individual and one that can be enjoyed in community. As God continues to unveil God's grace to all of creation, we find in Ephesians the intimate and intoxicating grace that compels people like the Apostle Paul. Paul often writes about how unworthy he is of God's grace, yet the inexhaustible God is always gracious and abundant. This individual calling radiates also to the Gentiles. Here we discover a costly grace compelling Paul to share with all people.

Focusing on the Second Prophet Isaiah in chapter 60, we move from an individual response to God's grace to the glowing effects of the presence of God.

> Arise! Shine! Your light has come;
> > the LORD's glory has shone upon you.
> Though darkness covers the earth
> > and gloom the nations,
> > the LORD will shine upon you;
> > God's glory will appear over you. (vv. 1-2)

Here we find wonderful imagery of the awesome presence of God that fills a city, children that return home. Imagine a home that is filled with the laughter of children and the effervescent glow of the Holy One. It's possible to tie these themes within Ephesians and Isaiah to the central theme found in Matthew of strangers who proclaim the birth of the Christ child.

Within these three texts the proclamation and effect of God comes from strangers; it happens in a deeply personal way or can fill a whole city with joy. Imagine how the Holy One is engaging in the lives of the people you are serving this week. How is God active in the seen and the unseen? How is the sacredness of God moving deeply within people yearning for an aha moment? Where is the light of Christ shining in the places you live, work, play, and learn?

Responsive Reading (Based on Psalm 72:1-7)

God, give your judgments to the king.

Give your righteousness to the king's son.

Let him judge your people with righteousness

and your poor ones with justice.

Let the mountains bring peace to the people;

let the hills bring righteousness.

Let the king bring justice to people who are poor;

let him save the children of those who are needy,

but let him crush oppressors!

Let the king live as long as the sun,

as long as the moon,

generation to generation.

Let him fall like rain upon fresh-cut grass,

like showers that water the earth.

Let the righteous flourish throughout their lives,

and let peace prosper until the moon is no more. Amen!

Benediction

May the incredible, insatiable love of the Holy One speak to your heart today. May you experience God through the blessing of someone unexpected. May you experience grace that touches your heart and changes your action. May your city and her children be filled with both laughter and grace today. Amen.

January 8, 2017

Isaiah 42:1-9; Psalm 29; Acts 10:34-43; Matthew 3:13-17

Gathering Prayer

God of all creation, prepare our hearts, minds, and very essence to encounter all that you are. We open ourselves to your teaching, to the activity of your Holy Spirit, to your faithfulness from generation to generation. We give you thanks for your love manifested through Jesus the Christ. May your will be done; may we listen attentively; may we follow accordingly. Amen.

Preaching Theme

In the Gospel of Matthew, there are so many rich themes to draw from: the sacrament of baptism, preparation for ministry, fulfillment of scripture, and the significance of family are just a few to name. A powerful theme within this text focuses on Jesus's preparation for formal ministry. To truly appreciate Jesus's and John's interaction, we must take a step back.

The sons of Elizabeth and Mary were related to one another. We can find that Mary spent time with Elizabeth during Elizabeth's last trimester and early in Mary's pregnancy. We don't know if this interaction in Matthew 3 is Jesus's first time meeting John face-to-face.

In the scriptures, we only find them interacting once, in this place located in the Jordan River. Here we find John, who is reaching the peak of his ministry, living in the margins of society calling for repentance in Yahweh's name. John has his own set of followers and disciples; we will explore this point in the next article. Next, we find Jesus, who is beginning the formal stage of his ministry, approaching his older cousin John.

What was the significance of John baptizing Jesus in the Jordan River as Jesus began his ministry? How do we discern which mentors, teachers, and spiritual leaders are the ones to follow? What does it mean for us to hear God's calling through mentoring and guidance of others? As we seek to discern God's calling for each of us, how do we know who to listen to and how to be in alignment with God's will?

Secondary Preaching Themes

Acts 10:34-43

In the Acts of the Apostles, Peter recounts the roles and relationships that John the Baptist and Jesus play. Just as John pointed toward the Messiah, Jesus continued his cousin's ministry by fulfilling the prophecies such as the one found in Isaiah 42.

Isaiah 42:1-9

The prophet Isaiah proclaims the coming of the Messiah. Unfortunately for the Hebrew people of Isaiah's day, the Messiah would not come in their lifetime. They would live and they would die still in a time of anticipation, of waiting. At the same time, however, the Hebrew people were also remembering the story of Yahweh's faithfulness throughout all generations. From their time as slaves in Egypt to the day when Yahweh's kingdom would come, the people held on to the faithfulness of their God. How do our places of worship yet today anticipate the coming of the Messiah? In what ways do we claim the risen Christ, who will come again, while still remembering God's faithfulness throughout the generations?

Responsive Reading (Based on Psalm 29:1-5, 10-11)

You, divine beings! Give to the LORD—

give to the LORD glory and power!

Give to the LORD the glory due his name!

Bow down to the LORD in holy splendor!

The LORD's voice is over the waters;

the glorious God thunders;

the LORD is over the mighty waters.

The LORD's voice is strong;

the LORD's voice is majestic.

The LORD's voice breaks cedar trees—

yes, the LORD shatters the cedars of Lebanon.

. . . .

The LORD sits enthroned over the floodwaters;

the LORD sits enthroned—king forever!

Let the LORD give strength to his people!

Let the LORD bless his people with peace! AMEN!

Benediction

May the God of yesterday, today, and tomorrow be with you. May the Holy One surround you with teachers, prophets, and mentors to help you listen attentively to God's faithful calling. May you begin and end this day seeking God's will. Amen.

January 15, 2017

Isaiah 49:1-7; Psalm 40:1-11; 1 Corinthians 1:1-9; John 1:29-42

Gathering Prayer

Holy One, we come before you as a people who deeply yearn to encounter and engage with you in a real and profound way. We confess to you that your presence was here long before we were ever aware. We acknowledge that our desire to stay comfortable sometimes comes at the cost of embracing your kingdom. May all that we are be attuned to all that you are doing right here and now. For you are God and we are not. Forgive us for the moments in our lives when we forget this profound truth. Amen.

Preaching Theme

In his book *Deep and Wide: Creating Churches Unchurched People Love to Attend*, megachurch pastor Andy Stanley wrote, "It takes great effort, vigilant leadership, and at times good, old-fashioned goading to keep a movement moving."[1] This quote keeps ringing in my mind as I reflect upon the interaction between John the Baptist and his disciples. That's right: *his* disciples.

It's an easily forgotten fact that John the Baptist had his own followers, his own disciples. Part of the reason why we don't even know their story with John is because once John encounters the Messiah, he immediately keeps the "movement moving" in the direction of Jesus. From John's perspective, he was kingdom-focused on what the Messiah was doing. Surely John had knowledge of the prophecies foretelling of the Messiah to come. What's amazing about John is that he wasn't just waiting for Jesus…he was expecting him!

How do we expect and anticipate that Jesus is coming again? Are our worship services, our planning and meetings steeped in the knowledge that Jesus is coming? If we don't live and act with anticipation…why not? What keeps us from fully letting go and completely living into the faithful belief that Jesus is coming? Are we willing to let go of *our* followers and disciples the way John did? Are our people prepared to meet Jesus on that sacred day? Why or why not?

Secondary Preaching Themes

1 Corinthians 1:1-9

In the letter to the early churches in Corinth, gratitude is the herb that steeps the tea of faith between the Apostle Paul and the early churches. As the early churches began to grow and flourish, it's entirely possible that one house church movement might find itself in competition with other house churches nearby. Quarreling over people who were already engaged in the early church is much like churches who compete over transfer members rather than nominal or unchurched neighbors.

While everyone is sacred in the eyes of God, how do we as the Christian movement continue to keep focused on keeping the irresistible gospel news of Jesus at the forefront of our mission and vision? To put it another way, how are we training disciples of Jesus really and truly to transform the world? How are we living and willing to share with gratitude the amazing ways that Jesus is at work in our lives individually and in the life of the church?

Isaiah 49:1-7

The context of the prophet's words in Isaiah 49 is significant. As earlier texts in Isaiah also stated, the Babylonian empire will fall to Cyrus. This noteworthy moment in history will in turn lead to the Hebrew people eventually becoming free from their exile, and this then leads to their ultimate restoration.[2] So the words of the ultimate servant bear incredible importance. In times when our nation is struggling, how might we as a people who want to be faithful to God remain true to our calling? In times of national stress and distress, how does our understanding of God's activity in our lives become focused? How might it change? What are some of the points of our faith that might be stretched when we feel as though we are in exile?

Benediction

May the God of one people and all nations draw you both closer to Godself and to all creation. May the peace of Christ be both still and active within your hearts, minds, and activities. May the grace of our Lord Jesus Christ guide you and keep you this day and forevermore. Amen.

January 22, 2017

Isaiah 9:1-4; Psalm 27:1, 4-9; 1 Corinthians 1:10-18; Matthew 4:12-23

Gathering Prayer

Creating, Redeeming, and Sustaining One, we confess to you that you are all that we need, our light and our hope. We confess that far too often we prefer our own ideologies above simply seeking your presence and guidance. We confess that we like to fill the air with lofty words rather than honest supplication. Free us to be a joyful and obedient people. This we ask in your Son's name, Jesus the holy and risen Christ. Amen.

Preaching Theme

In the Matthew text, Jesus chooses his first disciples as he propels himself into ministry. He calls Peter, Andrew, James, and John. The role of James and John in particular will be significant throughout the Gospel accounts, the two brothers often being remembered by their nickname: "the Sons of Thunder."

Just before the Passover meal, James and John were the two who argued over who would receive greater honor. James and John were there when Jesus revealed to his followers what was about to happen to him in Jerusalem. Instead of really trying to understand the meaning of Jesus's death, the brothers started to jockey for position, and to top it off they enlisted their mother to make a request on their behalf.

This conversation happened after three years of traveling with Jesus. These two men witnessed some of the most amazing moments in all of history. They were two of the very few witnesses who were on the mountain as they watched the transfiguration of Jesus. In Mark 5 they were allowed in Jarius's house to witness Jesus raising his daughter from the dead. In Mark 14, it was Peter, James, and John whom Jesus specifically asked to pray for him as he was in the garden of Gethsemane.

And yet, toward the end of Jesus's earthly ministry on earth, the Sons of Thunder lost focus on who they were following and why.

How are we remembering the amazing life, teachings, death, and resurrection of Jesus? How in our lives are we attentive to our personal desires for success, and are we aware of how this can pull us away from paying attention to God's kingdom plan to transform the world? In what ways are we shedding our ideologies and desires to keep aligned with servant leadership?

Secondary Preaching Themes

1 Corinthians 1:10-18

In Paul's letter to the early house churches in Corinth, it is clear that Paul is addressing a debate that had begun among the earliest Christian believers. Near as we can tell, these early Christians began to focus on their own desires and ideologies, pondering their own status and identity above their sacred calling to share the gospel of Jesus's good news first of all. In what ways do our faith communities seek to differentiate ourselves from other faith groups rather than focusing on the activity of the Holy Spirit here and now? What does it mean to seek the kingdom of God rather than build my own kingdom? When was the last time we were foolish for the gospel?

Isaiah 9:1-4

The Reverend Dr. Martin Luther King Jr. observed that so often we fight hate with hate, but it never works. We fight darkness by bringing in darkness of our own. It never works. Love casts out hate. Light drives out darkness. Isaiah knew this. Light does not seek out light; it hunts the darkness where it lives and shows the darkness its true nature. One may argue that the very essence of light is to drive out darkness, while darkness cowers from the light at every turn.

That is the imagery and activity of the Sacred One for the Hebrew people. Light that sheds fear and saturates the people with increased joy.

Responsive Reading (Based on Psalm 27:1, 4-8)

The LORD is our light and my salvation.

Should we fear anyone?

The LORD is a fortress protecting my life.

Should we be frightened of anything?

. . . .

I have asked one thing from the LORD—

it's all I seek

to live in the LORD's house all the days of my life,

seeing the LORD's beauty

and constantly adoring his temple.

Because he will shelter us in his own dwelling

during troubling times;

he will hide us in a secret place in his own tent;

he will set us up high, safe on a rock.

Now our head is higher than the enemies surrounding us,

and we will offer sacrifices in God's tent—

sacrifices with shouts of joy!

We will sing and praise the LORD.

LORD, listen to my voice when we cry out—

have mercy on me and answer me!

Come, our heart says, seek God's face.

LORD, we do seek your face!

Benediction

May the God of grace and peace be with you this day and every day. May your moments from this one till you rest tonight be filled with peace of God that makes little sense but satisfies completely. May the love of Jesus fill your hearts today. Amen.

January 29, 2017

Micah 6:1-8; Psalm 15; 1 Corinthians 1:18-31; Matthew 5:1-12

Responsive Call to Worship

LEADER: You have been called, my brothers and sisters...

PEOPLE: For those who have been called, both Jews and Gentiles, Jesus Christ is God's power and God's wisdom.

LEADER: The message of the cross is foolishness to those who are being destroyed.

PEOPLE: But it is the power of God for those of us who are being saved.

LEADER: Look at your situation when you were called, brothers and sisters! By ordinary human standards not many were wise, not many were powerful, not many were from the upper class.

PEOPLE: But God chose what the world considers foolish to shame the wise. God chose what the world considers weak to shame the strong.

LEADER: It is because of God that you are in Christ Jesus. He became wisdom from God for us.

PEOPLE: This means that he made us righteous and holy, and he delivered us.

LEADER: This is consistent with what was written: The one who brags should brag in the Lord!

PEOPLE: We make our boast in the Lord today!

Preaching Theme

One day, Jesus sat down on a mountain to teach. As he opened his mouth, he gave us a glimpse of God's kingdom, God's wisdom, God's economy. Today we realize that God's ways are completely different from the human standards of this world.

In Matthew 5:3, Jesus says, "Happy are people who are hopeless [or some translations say "poor in spirit"], because the kingdom of heaven is theirs." Our culture says,

"You can do it. Trust yourself. Rely on yourself. Help yourself." Jesus says "happy" are the ones who recognize their own inability to change themselves and depend on God for the most basic of necessities.

Jesus continues. "Happy are people who grieve because they will be made glad" (v. 4). We pity those who lose a loved one. We pity those who are sad, grieving, crying. Our human standards would say, "Blessed are those who never have anything bad happen to them or to anyone they love." But the comfort aspect of God's character can only be known in suffering. The God of comfort will make the grieving glad.

Our culture says "Happy are those who make a name for themselves. Happy are those who look out for number one." Jesus says, "Happy are people who are humble" (v. 5). They will be happy for they will inherit the earth. No one inherits something they work for or deserve. The humble will inherit what is God's to begin with.

The list goes on. "Happy are people who are hungry and thirsty for righteousness, because they will be fed until they are full" (v. 6). To be hungry and thirsty is to be uncomfortable. Happy is the one who painfully longs to be right with God and right with others for they will be satisfied.

"Happy are people whose lives are harassed because they are righteous" (v. 10). Human wisdom would call us to live so that others would esteem us. We think we should live in such a way that we would avoid harassment and insults. But "God chose what the world considers weak to shame the strong. And God chose what the world considers low-class and low-life—what is considered to be nothing— to reduce what is considered to be something to nothing" (1 Cor 1:27-28).

It is clear that God's ways are very different to the ways of this world. Will we value what God values? Or will we orient our lives around human standards? Which will we choose?

Secondary Preaching Themes

We live in a world of instant gratification. All the Beatitudes of Matthew 5 are about delayed gratification. None of them is exciting or enjoyable in the moment, and none of the blessings come right away. Being helpless, grieving, being hungry, being a peacemaker, being harassed . . . these are in no way easy. These are not pleasurable experiences. But somehow we can be happy, even when we are enduring them, because there is a blessing to come.

Psalm 15 exalts the one who does what is right, even if it is painful in the short-run. Blessed is the one who won't accept a bribe against an innocent person. Blessed is the one who keeps their promise even when it hurts. Micah 6:8 reminds us that what God is looking for and requiring is one who is willing to "do justice, embrace faithful love, and walk humbly with God." God's way is not the way of immediate gratification. God's way is not the easy way, but it is the best way.

Benediction

May you resist the tendency to submit yourself to ordinary human standards, but rather may you joyfully surrender to the ways of God, who is the author of all life. May you find happiness and blessedness in humility, in justice, and even in your own helplessness. And, may you look forward and live in light of your blessings that are to come.

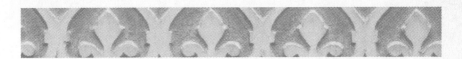

The Urgency of Now

Micah 6:1-8

Lia McIntosh

Rev. Dr. Martin Luther King Jr.'s Birthday

Good morning. We gather this morning to reflect on God and to remember the Rev. Dr. Martin Luther King's legacy of courage for our world today.

I speak to you not as an expert on Dr. King, but as a student. I share not as one who lived through the civil rights movement but as one who has benefited from the movement. I seek to keep Dr. King's legacy of love, service, and courage alive as a member of the Kansas City community, a pastor, and most importantly the mother of three children. Today is an occasion to *remember, celebrate, and act* in honor of God's work through the Rev. Dr. Martin Luther King Jr.

Let's start by remembering our collective history.

Nearly one hundred years after the Emancipation Proclamation of 1863, African Americans, especially those in Southern states, still lived in an unequal world of segregation and various forms of oppression, including race-inspired violence. "Jim Crow" laws at the local and state levels barred African Americans from classrooms and bathrooms, from theaters and voting booths, from juries and legislatures.

Finally, in 1954, the U.S. Supreme Court struck down the "separate but equal" laws that had allowed racial discrimination in schools with the decision of *Brown vs. the Board of Education.*

In the turbulent years that followed that important decision, civil rights activists used nonviolent protest and civil disobedience to bring about change, as seen in movies such as *Selma*, released in 2014. Through their action, the federal government finally enacted legislation such as the Voting Rights Act of 1965 and the Civil Rights Act of 1968.

Many leaders from within the African American community and beyond rose to prominence during the civil rights era, including Rev. Dr. Martin Luther King Jr. and Rosa Parks. In Kansas City many leaders such as Rev. Nelson "Fuzzy" Thompson, Congressman Emmanuel Cleaver II, and others risked—and sometimes lost—their lives in the name of freedom and equity. Today, we have a national holiday celebrating Dr. Martin Luther King Jr. because he gave his life for the freedom and equity of all humanity in America.

Let's take a moment, have a bit of fun, and quiz your civil rights history.

1. The 1955–56 Montgomery bus boycott, a protest against segregated public facilities in Alabama, was led by Dr. Martin Luther King Jr. and lasted for how many days? **381 days**

2. Dr. Martin Luther King Jr. realized that the nonviolent tactics used by this Indian political and religious leader was one of the most potent weapons available to African Americans in their struggle for freedom. Who was this Indian political and religious leader? **Mahatma Gandhi**

3. With the goal of redeeming "the soul of America" through nonviolent resistance, this organization was established in 1957, to coordinate the action of local protest groups throughout the South drawing on the power and independence of black churches to support its activities. What was this organization? **Southern Christian Leadership Conference (SCLC)**

4. During what event did Martin Luther King Jr. deliver his famous "I Have a Dream" speech?

   (A) The Selma campaign

   (B) The Birmingham campaign

   (C) The March on Washington—**Correct**

   (D) The Montgomery bus boycott

5. What was a common motto of civil rights activists in the 1950s and 1960s?

   (A) "We Shall Overcome"—**Correct**

   (B) "Liberty and Justice for All"

   (C) "One Nation Under God"

   (D) "Live and Let Live"

Did anyone get all five correct? Good job!

Today we often take our freedoms for granted. Yet, it is moments like today that must cause us to stop and remember the sacrifices that our foremothers and forefathers made for us. For that we give thanks.

Let me share a bit about my story.

I was born on November 1, 1972, four years after Dr. King was killed. My African American parents grew up during the civil rights movement.

My mother was raised in a segregated rural Mississippi community. Her family is documented in the Civil Rights Museum in Memphis, Tennessee, for their work in Mississippi registering African Americans to vote.

My father grew up in St. Louis, Missouri. As a college student, he was actively involved in integrating lunch counters in Kirksville, Missouri. Interestingly, he and a close friend were headed to Selma, Alabama, to participate in the 1964 civil rights march but never made it because the bus leaving from Kirksville was full and had no seats for them.

My parents' struggle and the sacrifices of many who followed Dr. King shaped the course of my life even before I was aware of its impact. Growing up a few miles from Ferguson, Missouri, in St. Louis County, I benefited from integrated schools and had many options to study, shop, and eat like many in this room.

And yet, today I realize that while we have progressed tremendously in the past fifty years, there is still great need for courageous leaders to advocate for civil rights. This is not just a race issue; it's a human issue.

Today, as the mother of three young children, I still have a dream that little black and brown boys and girls side by side with little white boys and girls will have equal access to excellent schools and to become world changers and history makers. I pray that they are judged not by the hoodies they wear or the natural texture of their hair, but by the content of their character. I am here today, because I believe there are many who are willing to keep working for this dream.

Martin Luther King Jr. and many others, outraged at the widespread injustices felt by African Americans, had the courage to confront those in power (both in the church and government), highlight abuses, and empower people by letting their voice be heard. Dr. King followed in the footsteps of prophets throughout the biblical scriptures who were spokespersons for God called to expose oppression and collective unrighteousness—that is injustice.

In our Old Testament text today, Micah prophesied to those in power, saying, "He has told you, human one, what is good and what the LORD requires from you: to do justice, embrace faithful love, and walk humbly with your God" (Mic 6:8).

Biblical prophets were uncompromisingly committed to justice for all, not just a few.

Biblical prophets exposed the sinful practices and policies that exploited and oppressed masses of people that religious and political leaders were tasked with serving.

Biblical prophets called for broad social reform, not just individual betterment for a few.

Biblical prophets afflicted the comfortable by challenging religious and political regimes to align with God's greater good.

So how do we prophesy for justice and carry the prophet Micah's and Dr. Martin Luther King's legacy of courage forward as people of faith today?

First, we serve others. As Jesus also did, so Dr. King often asked us to measure our lives by our service to friends and neighbors and strangers. How well do we serve others?

Each year, Americans across the country answer that question by coming together on the King holiday to serve their neighbors and communities. It's an opportunity for Americans from all walks of life to work together. May the King holiday be a day on, not a day off.

Second, we must learn the facts to determine whether injustices still exist today in our communities.

For example, education in America in some cases is still as separate and unequal as these statistics demonstrate.

Racial Disparities in High School Dropout Rates

- Half of the nation's African American and Latino students are dropping out of high school, with the most severe problems being in segregated high poverty schools.

- Of schools with minority populations of at least 50 percent, half have dropout rates over 40 percent.

- Of schools comprised of at least 90 percent minority students, two-thirds of these schools have dropout rates of more than 40 percent.[3]

Racial Disparities in Incarceration and Criminal Sentencing

- From 1980 to 2008, the number of people incarcerated in America quadrupled—from roughly 500,000 to 2.3 million people.

- African Americans now constitute nearly 1 million of the total 2.3 million incarcerated population.

- African Americans are incarcerated at nearly six times the rate of whites.[4]

These are just two examples of civil rights issues of today. We must know the facts and continue to work toward justice.

Third, we must lift our voice. We have power as we join together as a community to vote, run, and lead. We must not only cast our vote but also ensure everyone has access to vote regardless of their background. We must know and talk with our elected officials, government and community leaders about the challenges of our time. Together we can make our community and nation one that provides an opportunity for every person to thrive. In particular, we must be advocates for those who are voiceless by being courageous enough to run for political office, serve on boards and commissions, to help lead policies for a more equitable society. As Dr. King knew and as we all know, people everywhere want to be free. It's innate. It's deep within us all. That's why no one will remain under oppression for long if they can do anything about it.

Everyone can make a difference.

Fourth, we must be willing to take nonviolent direct action.

You may ask: "Why direct action today? Why sit-ins, marches, protests, and so forth? Isn't just talking a better path?" No. If you ever read Dr. King's now-famous "Letter from a Birmingham Jail," you know that he believed action—especially nonviolent action—is what leads to real change. Words alone don't get the attention of the people with the power.

May we all have the courage to participate in nonviolent direct action, as we feel called. May we seek to bring good news to the poor and deliverance to the oppressed, not to bow to the desires of those in power simply to avoid making waves, but rather to stand for what is filled with justice, kindness, and humility with God.

As a young girl I often wondered why my parents and teachers insisted I know African history as a supplement to biblical and American history. I was often more interested in other things like my friends and sports. What they taught me is that the human race is inextricably connected in all communities across time and geography.

So, we cannot sit idly by in Kansas City and not be concerned about what happens in Ferguson. We cannot ignore what happens in north Kansas City because we live south of the river. We cannot isolate ourselves from poverty, neither closer to home nor farther away.

May the prophet Micah's and Dr. King's courage challenge each of us today toward action as we

1. serve others,

2. learn the facts,

3. let our voice be heard, and

4. take nonviolent direct action when necessary.

And, may our children and grandchildren carry on a legacy of faith and courage for many generations to come.

Amen.

February 5, 2017

Isaiah 58:1-9a (9b-12); Psalm 112:1-9 (10); 1 Corinthians 2:1-12 (13-16); Matthew 5:13-20

Gathering Prayer

God of justice and mercy, we come before you today. We come to seek you. We desire knowledge of your ways. We want to be close to you. We come to call on you and to hear you answer. We long to know that you are here with us. May we honor you not only with our lips but with our hearts. May we honor you not only here in this place but in every place you send us.

Preaching Theme

Isaiah 58:1-9a presents a strong and clear example of meaningless worship. Like many of us, the people of Israel were doing all the right worshipful things (see verse 2), but they were also doing all kinds of other things that had absolutely no place in the life of a worshipper. Their worship and their lifestyle did not match. God says, "You quarrel and brawl, and then you fast" (v. 4). And God makes it clear that this is not what God desires.

Are we coming to worship to please ourselves or to please God? If we want to please him, he says in no uncertain terms that he wants worship that breaks the chains of injustice. He is a just God after all. He desires that we set free the mistreated. He wants a worship that is willing to share what we have with others. After all, he has been generous with us! He wants a worship that is hospitable. We should be ready to bring the homeless poor into our house and not keep suffering hidden from our families. After all, he has welcomed us into his house and called us his sons and daughters. When we worship in this way, God will respond. We will hear him say, "I'm here." What could be better?

The way we worship in here should affect the way we live out there. What difference does it make to our neighbors, our coworkers, our fellow students, our family members? What difference does it make to them how we worship here on Sundays if we don't live that same way throughout the week? We are to let our lights shine before people so they can see the good things we do. It is then, according to Matthew 5:16, that they will praise our Father in heaven.

Worship, true worship, is so much more than lifting our voices in song together in this sanctuary. We are called to so much more than simply praying prayers and speaking out the praises of our God. We dare not come into this place on Sundays and sing and say one thing but then go out and live something entirely different.

Secondary Preaching Themes

Matthew 5:17-20 and Psalm 112 both reveal the blessing that is connected to obeying God's commands. In Matthew, Jesus says that whoever keeps God's commands and teaches others to keep them as well "will be called great in the kingdom of heaven" (5:19). Psalm 112:1 says that those "who honor the Lord" and "who adore God's commandments, are truly happy!" There is the internal blessing of happiness. But, the blessing doesn't stop there. There is blessing for our families when we obey God. "The offspring of those who do right will be blessed" (v. 2). There is a blessing that endures. "Their righteousness stands forever" (v. 3). There is a blessing that overflows to those we meet. "They shine in the dark for others" (v. 4). There is a blessing of stability. "They won't be frightened at bad news. Their hearts are steady, trusting in the LORD" (v. 7).

Prayer of Confession

O God, you are always true to your word. What you say and what you do are in pure and perfect harmony. Forgive us for the times we have said one thing and done another. Forgive us for the times we have claimed to love you but have hated our brother or sister. Forgive us for the times we have sung songs here in church and had no intention of living them. Help us to see you for who you truly are. Help us to become more and more like you. Help us to value the things you value. And help us to obey your commands. In the name of Jesus, our Lord we pray. Amen.

Benediction

May what you have seen of God today affect the way you live your life tomorrow. May you know the happiness that is found in obeying God's commands. May you give freely to those in need. May you break the yokes of injustice. May your light shine in the darkness. May your light break out like the dawn. And may your strength increase gloriously and your righteousness stand forever. Amen.

February 12, 2017

Deuteronomy 30:15-20; Psalm 119:1-8; 1 Corinthians 3:1-9; Matthew 5:21-37

Preaching Theme

According to Deuteronomy 30:15-20, every day life and death, blessing and curse are set before us. Blessing is waiting for us if we would love the Lord, walk in his ways, and keep his commandments. Conversely, if our hearts turn away and refuse to listen and obey, it will mean death for us. What will we choose?

God's commands are for our well-being. Psalm 119:1-2 says that those "who walk in the LORD's Instruction—are truly happy! Those who guard God's laws are truly happy! They seek God with all their hearts." Following God's commands brings happiness and wholeness to our bodies. But the blessing God desires for us goes deeper than that. God desires that our hearts be at rest and whole.

In Matthew 5, Jesus makes it clear that he takes God's commands to another level: "You have heard that it was said…, Don't commit murder.…But I say to you that everyone who is angry with their brother or sister will be in danger of judgment.…If they say, 'You fool,' they will be in danger of fiery hell" (vv. 21-22). It is not simply about refraining from killing someone else. It is about being careful to care for their hearts and to take care that anger and malice are not in control of our own hearts.

Every day we choose. Every moment we choose. Will we choose life or death? Will we disobey God and reap the destructive consequences in our minds, bodies, hearts, and relationships? Or will we obey God's commands and receive the blessing he offers? God desires to bless us. God desires that we would not merely survive, but that we would thrive.

Secondary Preaching Theme

Each one of us has a role given to us by the Lord. Some plant, some water. We don't get to decide what our role is. There is blessing for us if we will gladly accept the role that God gives us. There is joy for us when we stop comparing ourselves to others and wishing we could do what someone else does. It is up to the wisdom of our God. First Corinthians 3:1-9 says that some plant, some water, but God makes growth happen. We do our jobs, but truly, apart from God's working, our best efforts are worthless. "Neither the one who plants nor the one who waters is anything, but the only one who is anything is God who makes it grow" (v. 7). We don't have to make everything happen. It is not our job. We must release ourselves from that kind of pressure. We must be faithful to do what God has given us to do. We will receive our own reward for our own labor. And, we can delight in the reality that the almighty God of the universe allows each of us to play a unique part in his work.

Responsive Confession

ALL: Most Holy God, your ways are right and true. Your statutes are life and peace. You have ordered that your statutes be kept most carefully.

LEADER: You have commanded us not to murder. You have also commanded us that we must not use our words to harm or insult others.

PEOPLE: How I wish my ways were strong when it comes to keeping your statutes! I am often careless with my words and speak things that do not build up and benefit others.

LEADER: You have commanded us that we should make our relationships right before we come to worship you and offer you our gifts.

PEOPLE: How I wish my ways were strong when it comes to keeping your statutes! Often, I come to worship you knowing that I have something against my brother or sister.

LEADER: You have commanded us to let our "yes" be "yes" and our "no" be "no."

PEOPLE: How I wish my ways were strong when it comes to keeping your statutes! I have not kept all my promises to myself, to others, or to you.

LEADER: God, you have ordered that your decrees should be kept most carefully.

PEOPLE: I will keep your statutes. Please don't leave me all alone!

Benediction

May you be content to be who God has called you to be. May you trust God's wisdom and plan. May you believe in your soul that God's commands are for your benefit. May you know that God has your best interest at heart. May you cling to God tightly so that you will be able to obey faithfully. May you walk joyfully in God's ways and seek the Lord with all your heart. Amen.

February 19, 2017

Leviticus 19:1-2, 9-18; Psalm 119:33-40; 1 Corinthians 3:10-11, 16-23; Matthew 5:38-48

Gathering Prayer

Jesus, Son of God, thank you for putting on flesh and becoming our neighbor. You did not have to treat us with such kindness, but you did. You gave yourself unselfishly to us when we were living in complete selfishness. Thank you for loving us when we gave you no reason. We want to be loving as you are loving. We want to give to others who would least expect it. Help us to be generous for no other reason than that you have been generous with us. Help us to be the kinds of neighbors that we would hope others would be for us.

Preaching Theme

The call of a Christian is first and foremost a call to love. In fact, Jesus himself said that others would know that we are his disciples by the love that we show. We are called to love because we have been loved. And, the truth is, we have been loved when we were not at all lovely. The Bible tells us that while we were sinners, indeed while we were enemies of God, Christ died for us. And it is this kind of love that we are called to show. We are called to offer to others the kind of love we have received. We are called to love in unexpected, extravagant ways. We are called to love the people who might least expect it. And we are called to love not merely by our words but by practical action.

In Leviticus 19, ten verses are devoted to specifically lining out practical ways to love our neighbors as we love ourselves. And our neighbors might be those who normally get overlooked or even mistreated. We are called to love the poor and the immigrant by not taking all we could take of our own produce. We are to leave some for them to glean. We are to love our employees by paying them quickly. We are to treat the deaf and the blind with respect.

We are to love our neighbors no matter who they may be. But in Matthew 5:38, Jesus, as he often does, takes it a step further. He calls us to love our enemies. He calls us to love the people who treat us unjustly by praying for them. He calls us to love the people who would steal from us by offering them more than what they demand from us. He calls us to go the extra mile and to give freely, for we have freely received so much more than we deserved.

Secondary Preaching Theme

In both Matthew and Leviticus, we are encouraged to leverage the element of surprise. It is not stated in the texts, but it is there underlying. Someone who is stealing from us would never expect us to offer more than they demand. A poor immigrant would never expect a wealthy business owner to consider him. A deaf person and a blind person would expect to be overlooked, if not completely mistreated. The one who hits us on one cheek would not imagine that we would offer the other cheek as well. The kind of love that we are called to is unexpected because it is not natural. It is supernatural.

Dramatic Reading

READER #1: Before you could ever return it...
READER #2: Before you could try hard to earn it...
READER #3: Before you could fail to deserve it...
ALL: You were loved.

READER #2: Before you could ever explain it...
READER #3: Before you could try to contain it...
READER #1: Before you could fail to attain it...
ALL: You were loved.

READER #1: Long before you were...
READER: #2: Wrong
READER #1: Long before you were...
READER #3: Right
ALL: You were loved.

Benediction

You are loved extravagantly. Know it deep down inside.

You were loved before you could even try to earn it. Receive the unconditional love God has for you. And as you receive God's love...

May you love others before they have a chance to earn your love.

May you surprise others with love in practical ways when they least expect it.

May you love those who normally get ignored.

And may you, even as Jesus did, treat your enemies with a kindness and generosity they do not deserve.

February 26, 2017
Transfiguration Sunday

Exodus 24:12-18; Psalm 2; 2 Peter 1:16-21; Matthew 17:1-9

Gathering Prayer

Almighty and loving God, come and be with us as we worship on this Transfiguration Sunday. We pray for greater insight into the guiding lights of your Son Jesus and how that transfiguration is to be a part of who we are in Christ Jesus. We are open and willing to maintain our understanding of the Law and Prophets in the Old Testament as we have moved to receive Jesus in the New Testament. Thank God for his guiding lights. May we receive you among us and in us. May we always know your touch and honor your glory. In Jesus's name we pray. Amen.

Preaching Theme

The Greek *metamorphoō* means transfigured, transformed, changed in form. It is a transformation from the inside that reveals itself on the outside. Scripture tells us that Jesus took Peter, James, and John to a mountain where they witnessed this event. His face was like the light of the sun, his clothes like a bright light. While Jesus took them to the top of a mountain, it was God who commanded Moses to go to the top of a mountain where he would receive the tablets upon which the Ten Commandments were written.

The bright light reminds us of the pillars of cloud and fire that guided the children of Israel out of Egypt. The Lord our God appears in these guiding lights as the God who is with us wherever we go in our life journey. The clouds and fires represent the presence of God in front of us, guiding us by day and night (Exod 13:20-22).

The transfiguration of Jesus is seen as a divine light that emanated from his body that revealed to the disciples truths they had not understood through Jesus's words alone. Jesus knew they would not be able to comprehend the resurrection, so they were provided with the unforgettable visual teaching method. The hardest lessons that we learn in life stay with us because we witness them with our eyes. As humans, we believe what we see and not what others see for us. Jesus knew that the coming events of his suffering, death, and resurrection would become the "good news" throughout eternity if told through the eyes and memory of the disciples.

There the disciples saw Jesus's face and clothing shine bright while talking to Moses and Elijah. Jesus was talking to them about his death, which would happen soon. While Peter did not know what was being discussed, he innocently offered to make a shrine for each of them. God's voice was heard from a bright cloud over them saying, "This is my Son whom I dearly love. I am very pleased with him. Listen to him" (Matt 17:5). The disciples fell to the ground and hid their faces until Jesus told them "don't be afraid" (v. 7). When they opened their eyes, Jesus was standing alone. These words are familiar to us when God said, "You are my son" (Ps 2:7) because these were the words God used when Jesus was baptized by water and the Spirit.

God, our Creator, understands everything about us, and therefore knows how to teach us and guide us, just like he did with the Israelites and the disciples.

Secondary Preaching Themes

In the text 2 Peter 1:16-21 we find that God's teaching method remains with Peter, who boldly confronts and argues with false teachers that Jesus will return. The belief of the second coming is held tightly by Peter mainly because he was an eyewitness to the glory of God and Jesus's transfiguration. Peter knew as an eyewitness the truth of God's majesty and strongly stated that he was not telling false tales. He speaks in first person and also in third person, using the other witnesses to validate what Jesus had communicated to them through the transfiguration, what they heard and saw. They heard God give honor to his Son and saw glory in the brightness of Jesus's face and clothing. They saw and heard the honor and glory of Jesus, for Jesus is identified as the Messiah of Israel, and the coming of his future kingdom.

The witness of the apostles is the foundation of our faith.

Responsive Reading (Based on Psalm 99)

May the grace and love of God and the fellowship of the Holy Spirit be with you.

And also with you.

Great is the lord in Zion.

He is exalted over all of the nations.

God is All Powerful.

God answered the prayers of Moses and Aaron, and he spoke to them through pillars of clouds and fire.

God is Holy.

Let everyone worship him now and forever.

Benediction

Go forth and serve in the foundation of our faith, knowing the honor and glory of Jesus. And may the peace of God be with you now and forever. In the name of the Father, and of the Son, and of the Holy Spirit. Amen.

After Meeting Glory

Exodus 24:12-18

Ted A. Smith

Transfiguration Sunday

Today is the day that the church remembers the transfiguration of Jesus. We remember how he went up on the mountain with his closest disciples, how his face shone with the glory of the Lord, how the disciples knew just enough to be afraid. And we remember the story that was deep in the memories of the Gospel writers, the story of Moses on Mount Sinai.

God calls Moses to come up the mountain. Moses—like a good, responsible pastor—delegates his duties while he is away. He tells people they can take disputes to Aaron and Hur. And then he goes up the mountain. The glory of the Lord settles on the mountain, Exodus says. A cloud covers it for six days. Moses waits in base camp. And then, on the seventh day, God calls to Moses from the cloud. Moses goes into the cloud. Into the cloud. He beholds the glory of the Lord. Exodus does not tell us what Moses sees. But the people at the foot of the mountain see a devouring fire. And Moses stays in that fire, with the glory of the Lord, for forty days.

Today's lesson ends there. But it is worth remembering what comes next, what comes *after meeting glory*. After Moses has been gone for forty days and forty nights, the people begin to wonder if he will ever return. Just as Moses told them to, they take their concerns to Aaron. With Moses gone, and no one knowing when or if he's ever coming back, the people ask for new representations of God's presence with them. Aaron gathers up all the gold they took with them from Egypt and cast for them a golden calf. The people made offerings before it. And so they break their covenant with God. But their minds are at ease. (Idolatry has that effect on us.)

You know what happens next, maybe from seeing Charlton Heston enact the wrath of God. Moses storms down the mountain, sees the people reveling before the golden calf. He shatters the tablets written with the finger of God, the tablets God had given him to mark the covenant. He calls out, "Whoever is on the LORD's side, come to me!" (32:26). The Levites respond. He tells them to draw their swords, slaughter the idolaters, and ordain themselves to the priesthood in the blood of their kinfolk.

After meeting glory, Moses becomes a religious extremist. He kills his own people for breaking faith with God. Moses is not the first to kill in the name of God. He will not be the last. Seeing all this blood, over all these centuries, many contemporary commentators argue that we should not go up the mountain at all. Because after people meet the glory of God, they too often kill people who have met a different god, or no god at all. It would be better, these critics say, to stay on the plain with the people, to work things out in the secular key of workaday politics. For when people go up the mountain, when they meet the glory of God, or think they do, they become dangerous.

For those of us who put our trust in God, or long to, it can be tempting to ignore this part of the story. We might follow the lead of the lectionary, telling the story of the glory of God while trying to forget what happens after meeting glory. But I think we've got to remember this story. It can both chasten and guide us.

Let's slow down to read it all more closely. It's in Exodus 32, if you want to read along. When God hears the children of Israel reveling before the calf, God gets furious. God tells Moses to go down—go down, just as he had to Egypt—only this time, not to free the people but to destroy them. "Leave me alone!" God says. "Let my fury burn and devour them" (v. 10). God wants to wipe out the children of Israel and start a new covenant people from Moses and his descendants.

Moses pleads with God on behalf of Israel. He tries every kind of persuasive appeal he can. "Why should the Egyptians say 'He had an evil plan to take the people out and kill them in the mountains and so wipe them off the earth?'" (v. 12). And the clincher—"Remember Abraham, Isaac, and Israel, your servants, whom you yourself promised 'I'll make your descendants as many as the stars in the sky'" (v. 13). Abraham's pleas move God. And, Exodus 32:14 says, in one of the most remarkable passages in scripture, God changes God's mind. Not because the people apologized. Not because they turned away from the calf. Not because God thinks they will do better in the future. It has nothing to do with who they are or what they do. It has everything to do with who God is—a faithful God—and what God does—keep God's promises.

This is crucial to remember. Before Moses takes one step down the mountain, God has forgiven the people. God has chosen to keep the covenant that the people tried to break. Because of God's own character, God has decided not to destroy them.

If you want to see the full glory of the Lord, it is here. The fullness of God's glory comes not in beautiful blue pavements or thrones or even all-consuming fires. The glory of *this* God, the God of Abraham and Sarah, the God we know in Jesus Christ, is manifest in this moment when God decides not to destroy the people but to take into God's own self the cost of their chasing after idols. God decides to keep faith with a people who do not keep faith with God. Behold, the glory of the Lord!

Moses pleads for that glory. He prays for it. But he cannot live with it. When he goes down the mountain, when he sees the idolatry of the people, he becomes hot with anger. No one can talk him out of it. And so he calls for blood.

We must not miss the irony here. Moses had pleaded for the people, God had forgiven them just as Moses had begged God to do . . . and then Moses slaughtered people in just the way that he asked God not to do. In this violence Moses did what God had decided not to do. He let his own decision trump God's decision. He shattered the tablets that were a sign of the covenant God had decided to keep. He avenged a God who had forsworn vengeance. In making a decision that was God's to make and taking action that was God's to take, Moses put himself in the place of God. And here is the irony: in putting himself in the place of God, Moses replaces God with something less than God. This is idolatry. Moses has people killed for worshipping the golden calf. But exactly in striking out against idolatry, Moses becomes an idolater.

The lesson of Sinai is not fundamentalism. It is not that we should take vengeance on idolaters, as if God needed us to execute God's judgments. But neither is the lesson of Sinai a kind of secularism. It is not that we should never go up the mountain, lest God demand violence of us. The lesson of Sinai is that God keeps faith even with the faithless—even with people who worship golden calves, or personal security, or individual wealth, or social status, or thin bodies, or political power. The lesson of Sinai is that God keeps faith not only with those we despise but also with us.

To say that God keeps faith with us does not mean that God does not care what we do. It does not mean that anything goes. After all, God's keeping faith with Israel involved giving again the tablets of the Law that Moses had destroyed. God loves us too much to leave us to our own devices.

The church year teaches us something in putting Transfiguration Sunday right before Lent. After meeting the glory of a God who keeps faith with the faithless, we should not come down the mountain to avenge a God who has renounced revenge. We should rather come down the mountain full of confidence in God's love for the very people who have betrayed God, even ourselves. After meeting glory, we should be moved to repent of the idolatries God has already forgiven. After meeting glory, we should come down the mountain ready to engage in the difficult discipleship of loving the people God has decided to love. After meeting glory, we should prepare to journey with Jesus to the cross that is the price of this love. After Transfiguration, Lent. And after meeting glory, we journey to the cross.

March 5, 2017
First Sunday of Lent

Joel 2:1-2, 12-17; Psalm 32; Romans 5:12-19; Matthew 4:1-11

Gathering Prayer

Almighty God, we thank you this day for the amazing way that your Son Jesus used his free will and resisted the temptations of the devil. We pray that we may walk in his path every day giving you honor and glory. May we grow in righteousness that is acceptable to you. In Jesus's name we pray. Amen.

Preaching Theme

Our lives and the world are full of temptations. Even when we are living a good life, we allow our attention to be taken off of God and redirected to wrongdoing. Jesus, Son of God, came and experienced the challenges of temptation that prevents us from living godly lives. Temptations come from a source known as the tempter, the devil or Satan. Regardless of the name we know it by, all tests can be defeated by God as Jesus revealed to us. Jesus came to understand the world we live in and the choices that are constantly in front of us. Perhaps that is why the Holy Spirit led Jesus to the wilderness for forty days and forty nights. Jesus came to understand our human brokenness and frailty through the forty days of temptations, and his experiences reflect what we face every day too.

Jesus had fasted for forty days and so was very hungry when the devil's first temptation commanded that Jesus turn stones into bread. Even though the devil was appealing to Jesus's personal satisfaction, Jesus replied, "It's written, *People won't live only by bread, but by every word spoken by God*" (Matt 4:4). Jesus refused to make his personal needs the center of his life but continued to focus on God's plans and trust God. Jesus teaches us to resist temptation for *personal reasons*. The next temptation was when the devil stood Jesus at the highest point of the temple and instructed him to throw himself down so that he could command the angels to keep him from hitting his foot on a stone. Jesus replied, "*Don't test the Lord your God*" (v. 7). Jesus was not tempted to use *sensationalism* to attract attention. Again Jesus refused to put himself in front of God.

Then the devil took Jesus to a high mountain and showed him all of the kingdoms and offered them to him if he would bow and worship him. Jesus replied, "*You will worship the Lord your God and serve only him*" (v. 10). Jesus resists the temptation of power and control and again uses free will to resist temptation. We have learned from Jesus that he really knows what it is like to be tempted. With the strength of the word of God and faith, we can defeat temptation.

Secondary Preaching Themes

The text in Romans 5:12-19 speaks of the temptation that took place in the garden of Eden where the serpent succeeded in convincing Adam and Eve to ignore God's instructions to not eat the fruit from the tree of knowledge because God was saving the best for Godself. Here the devil dangled the freedom of choice in front of them and caused them to fall. When we as humans accept the devil's temptation to not follow God's instructions, we are saying that God is not the center of our lives, and so we follow our desires and not God's will. When Adam and Eve accepted the temptation of the serpent, they created the *original sin*, which was inherited by all humankind. In contrast, Jesus's refusal to sin gave honor and glory to God the Father through acts of obedience, giving *justification* to all humankind.

In the text of Psalm 32, David tells us that the blessedness from God comes when we make a conscious effort to follow certain duties, which include following the instruction and teaching of God as to the ways we are to walk in life. Although David embraced the temptation with Bathsheba, he came to realize that the cost of accepting such a temptation was far greater than he could have ever imagined.

And finally, we see in the book of Joel, that their experiences with the locust changed when they repented and asked God to change the direction of God's people if they turn back toward God who is, "merciful and compassionate, / very patient, full of love" (Joel 2:13).

Responsive Reading

L: We serve a gracious and merciful God.

P: Let us be glad and rejoice.

L: He gave us Jesus so we are free from sin and enslavement.

P: We are glad in the Lord and give thanks that the Son of God has set us free.

L: Come, worship the Lord and serve him with glad hearts.

P: We will only worship and serve the Lord our God.

Benediction

With the love and power of the Holy Spirit, go forth and share with all men of all nations that Jesus defeated temptations and even death. With the strength of the word of God and faith, we can defeat temptation.

Jesus and Mosquito Bites

Matthew 4:1-11

O. Wesley Allen Jr.

In *The Color Purple*,[1] Alice Walker presents a conversation between Celie and Shug that is worthy of the halls of Perkins School of Theology, the seminary at which I teach. The two women are walking through a field of purple flowers, and the beauty of the sight raises for them the issue of the nature of God. Shug suggests that God made the flowers so beautiful because, more than anything, God loves admiration. When Celie asks her if that means God is vain, Shug answers by saying, "Naw." She continues, "Not vain, just wanting to share a good thing. I think it [makes] God [angry] if you walk by the color purple...somewhere and don't notice it."[2]

Did you notice? The white of Christmas is ancient past. The green of Epiphany has been folded and hung in the closet. Purple has appeared in their place. It slipped in on Wednesday when we are usually only here for supper, so it might be easy to have gone unnoticed. And if I hadn't called your attention to it today, you'd still have forty days ahead of us to take notice. You see, Lent is all about taking notice.

But taking notice of what? That's the question. Surely it's more than just taking notice of God's gift of purple. It's taking notice of God's gift of...Well, maybe it's best to enter from the side door.

Lent began in the early church as a period of preparation for baptism of converts. These converts would study the Bible and the faith intensely, they would pray constantly, and they would fast rigorously. It was a time to test out whether you really wanted to be a Christian or not. Do I really believe this stuff? Do I really want to live this Christian life? It is supposed to be different from the way other people live, you know. When you have faith in Christ and live in Christ, your life in the world doesn't buy into all the rhetoric about what a good worldly life is all about. So Lent evolved as a period for converts to try on the clothes of the Christian and see how they fit for a while before you decided to take that step on Easter and be baptized into wearing Christ forever. You know, in the early church they symbolized that by stripping naked before getting into the baptismal waters and then being clothed in a new white robe when they stepped out. Doing that in front of the whole church takes some guts, some real commitment. Maybe you ought to consider that whole naked thing next time someone is baptized here. Lent was a time for testing out whether you were ready for the kind of commitment and vulnerability it takes to be a Christian.

It's no wonder then that the early church used the story of Jesus's temptation as the lens for interpreting this trial period. One thing you might notice about the story is that Lent seems to get the order backward. We test out the faith before deciding to commit. But in the Gospels, Jesus is baptized and then has his faith tested. But let's be clear. In the story, Jesus isn't someone who is lost like Hansel and Gretel and accidentally stumbles upon Satan's gingerbread house out in the wilderness. Satan doesn't sing a Siren's song that seduces Jesus into coming out to the wilderness. No, indeed, the Holy Spirit comes upon Jesus after his baptism and then this very Spirit that has come from God, that is somehow God, *leads* Jesus into the wilderness to be tested by the devil. There is intentionality here. Jesus doesn't just happen to be tested when he is in the wilderness; he goes out there *in order to be tempted*. I mean, for heaven's sake, he fasts for forty days *so that* he will be tempted.

That's where it comes from, you know. Lenten discipline, that is. Modeled on Jesus fasting for forty days while being tempted by the devil. During Lent we abstain from something insignificant that we desire (chocolate, soft drinks, television, wine for time for prayer, Bible study, or volunteer work) *so that* we will be tempted to desire it all the more. Lent is temptation practice, if you will. We take on small temptations to rehearse for times when serious temptation comes knocking at our door and rattling our windows. We take on small disciplines so that we are ready for those hard, trying times in life when only self-discipline can get us through. To use an image from my home country of Alabama, Lent is like intentionally letting yourself get bitten by mosquitoes *so that* you can practice resisting the temptation to scratch when you get a bad case of poison ivy. Notice I didn't say *if* you get a bad case of poison ivy. I said *when*. In Alabama, everyone stumbles into poison ivy now and then. It's everywhere. It's unavoidable. But if you scratch you will make it so much worse. When you don't have the self-discipline not to scratch it, you spread it around with your fingertips. It moves from the back of your hand, all up your arm; it shows up on your cheek; it gets inside your eye. In Lent we allow ourselves to be bitten by mosquitoes so that we can practice not scratching while the itch is fairly mild so that we will be able to resist scratching when the itch is almost unbearable.

So what is this bad case of poison ivy for which we prepare in Lent? What is the real temptation for which we're rehearsing? Matthew provides an answer.

Now I know we've all heard sermons on the story of Jesus's temptation that look at each temptation separately. First, there's the temptation to turn stones into bread. Second, if he were to jump down from the steeple on top of the temple in Jerusalem, God would prevent him from even stubbing his toe and everyone would believe. And third, Satan promises that if Jesus worships him for just a moment, he will give to him authority over all the kingdoms of the world. Physical desire, the quest for power, and the lure of glory. Heck, it's a ready-made three-point sermon if I've ever heard one in my life. All preachers have to do is add two jokes and a poem, and they're ready to fly.

But actually, to walk through each movement of the story and separate them out as different temptations is to risk not seeing Jesus's wilderness for the trees. The three different tests are really only different on the surface. Down deep where the soul is touched, there is only one temptation—one temptation that manifests itself in millions of different ways.

Listen to the first words the tempter speaks to Jesus: "If you are the Son of God..." (Matt 4:3 NRSV). Those words echo back to Jesus's baptism, where the Spirit of God descends upon him, and the voice from heaven says, "This is my Son, whom I dearly love; I find happiness in him" (Matt 3:17). Immediately upon hearing these words at baptism, Jesus is led by the Spirit into the wilderness. And the next words he hears are, "If you are the Son of God, command these stones to become loaves of bread" (4:3 NRSV). The second temptation begins exactly the same way: "If you are the Son of God, throw yourself down" (v. 6 NRSV).

This is my Son...If you are the Son of God...

The focus here isn't so much on satisfying hunger or on performing miracles for show or on gaining political power as it is on the temptation for Jesus to act in a way that denies his identity as God's child. Of course, Matthew uses the title "Son of God" not just to speak of Christ's divine origins, but also to refer to his divine mission, because Jesus's identity and mission can't be separated. Jesus comes from God as God's child *in order to* serve God's people. Jesus is to meet the hungering needs of those whom society is either unable or unwilling to help. Jesus is to confront those religious authorities who are more concerned with the religious institution than with compassion and justice. Jesus is to preach about the dominion of God over against the dominions of the world in a way that calls those willing to hear the message to a posture of repentance. Jesus is to suffer, die, and be raised for those who follow, for those who forsake, for those who are forlorn, and for those who need forgiveness. The temptation Jesus faces in the wilderness is to turn away from the calling he received in his baptism.

This is what God gets angry about if we pass through our baptism and fail to notice: that God calls us. In theological lingo the word is vocation, but when we hear that we usually think about career choices. Vocation in the church isn't about *what* you want to be when you grow up; it's about *who* God calls us to be in every moment of our existence—at work, at school, at home, at church, at the gas station, at the basketball game, at the quilting bee...well, you get the idea. In baptism God calls us to the vocation of being Christian everywhere and all the time. Temptation doesn't simply challenge what we are going to do in this or that circumstance. It's not just, am I going to cheat on my taxes, cheat on my spouse, cheat on my homework? Temptation makes us question who we are...or better, *whose* we are. Temptation challenges us to cheat on being Christian, to cheat our very God-given identity.

In baptism God speaks to us and says, *"You are my child."* This is both claiming and calling for Christians. But it's not that God only says it once. It echoes through every prayer we utter when we believe God cares: "You are my child." It echoes through every sermon you hear preached in this place: "You are my child." It echoes through the Lord's Supper: "This is my body. This is my blood. *You* are my child." Thank heavens we have heard God claim and call us.

I say "thank heavens," because once we've heard it, once we know it, once we believe it, once we choose to wear the label "Christian," we are protected from ever being tempted again. That's right: we Christians are never again tempted the way the rest of the human race is tempted. Being persons of faith protects us from real, root-level temptation. After all, we will never be tempted in a time of economic recession to be concerned about our well-being while neglecting the needs of those who are poor and hungry. *If you are a child of God, then...*

We'll never be tempted to determine our self-worth by how much money we make or what grades we earn or who we marry or what job title we have. *If you are a child of God, then...*

We'll never be tempted to mistake the church building for the church in mission. *If you are a child of God, then…*

We'll never be tempted to allow our love for our nation to distort our claims about God's love for all God's people. *If you are a child of God, then…*

We'll never be tempted to laugh at a joke that demeans someone different than us, whether they be gay, or blond, or black, or old, or Jewish. *If you are a child of God, then…*

We'll never be tempted in our prayers to transform the creator of the universe into a Santa Claus who should be at our beck and call. *If you are a child of God, then…*

We'll never be tempted to look at the problems that show up on the evening news and say, "I am only one person, what can I do?" *If you are a child of God, then…*

We will never be tempted to feel jealous of churches that have something we don't or boastful before churches that do not have what we do. *If you are a child of God, then…*

We will never be tempted to put our family, our job, our schoolwork, our possessions, our church, our love for Kentucky basketball, our bank account, our country, our beliefs, or ourselves before God. *If you are a child of God, then…*

We who are called Christian, we whom God calls, are constantly tempted to forget *who* we are, to forget *why* we are, to forget *whose* we are. Lent is not as fun as Christmas—we don't have any Lenten carols. Lent is not as fun as Easter—no Lenten sunrise services. But *we* need Lent. We need time to rehearse with small temptations, so that we are ready when louder, more persuasive temptations come along. We need Lent to remind us of our daily vocation of being a Christian. We need Lent to help us notice once again and strive to live out the promise implicit in God saying to each of us every moment of our lives, "This is my Son whom I dearly love; I find happiness in him."

Parker Palmer tells a story about how similar the voices of temptation and the voice of God sound when it comes to defining who and whose we are.[3] Since the beginning of his adult career, he had had people telling him that someday he would be a college president. One day the opportunity finally came. A school made him an offer, but before he formally accepted he decided to follow the Quaker tradition and gather a group of trusted friends to serve as a clearness committee. The way such a committee works in the Quaker tradition is to gather for a few hours in which the committee members ask questions of but give no advice to the person seeking discernment. The thing about it is that Palmer admits that he wasn't really looking for discernment so much as it was a chance to brag a little.

Anyway, the clearness committee began by asking Palmer questions like: What's your vision for the school? How would you change the curriculum? How will you deal with conflict?

Then someone asked the simple question: "What would you like most about being a college president?" And Palmer began to say things like, "Well, *I wouldn't like* having to give up writing and teaching…And I wouldn't like the politics of the job…And I wouldn't like glad-handing people so they would give money to the school…And I wouldn't like…" And the questioner interrupted Palmer and reminded him, "I asked what you *would* like most." And Palmer said, "Yes, I'm working toward that. I wouldn't like having to give up my summer vacations…And I wouldn't like having to wear a suit all the time…And I wouldn't like…" And again the questioner asked, "What would you *like* most?" Parker thought, and all he could come up with was, "Well, I guess what I'd like most is getting my picture in the paper with the word *president* under it."

There followed a long, awkward, painful silence. Finally, the same questioner broke the silence and asked a follow-up question, a baptismal question, a Lenten question: "Parker, can you think of an easier way to get your picture in the paper?"[4]

Clearness committee [hold out one hand]. Lent [hold out other hand]. Temptation practice. Don't pass by purple without noticing. Don't pass by without noticing God calling us to the Christian life. Practice—don't scratch. Whose are you?

March 12, 2017
Second Sunday of Lent

Genesis 12:1-4a; Psalm 121; Romans 4:1-5, 13-17; John 3:1-17

Gathering Prayer

Almighty God, we repent of our sins and open our hearts to Jesus. We repent and believe in Jesus Christ as our Lord and Savior. We receive you in heart, body, and soul. Thank you for being with us both day and night as we search for light in dark places in this world. We pray to be obedient by waiting on your time schedule and responding according to your command. Thank you for the gift of salvation. In Jesus's name. Amen.

Preaching Theme

Many of us can recall the name of a good teacher who provided us with solid foundations in this or that school subject. But can we recall the name of a person who was a good teacher in the subject of life? Nicodemus, a member of the Jewish Council and a known Pharisee, pays a night visit to Jesus and states, "Rabbi, we know that you are a teacher who has come from God, for no one could do these miraculous signs unless God is with him" (John 3:2). He came at night because he was searching for answers or light in the dark places of his life. He also wanted to avoid being judged by his colleagues since this was a time when many were very bitter toward Jesus. At this time, Nicodemus spoke of how he was impressed with the signs that Jesus made, but Jesus moved to a more important subject when he stated that one must be, "born anew" (v. 3) before he can see the reign of God. A new life—like a brand-new baby discovering the world again. In those days and perhaps in today's society, where you come from determines who you are and where you are going. Jesus was clear that to be born again is to be connected or born from God "above." Nicodemus asked, "How is it possible for an adult to be born? It's impossible to enter the mother's womb for a second time and be born" (v. 4). Jesus said that since Nicodemus was a teacher, he should understand these things. It's all in scripture. Why couldn't Nicodemus see it?

To be born again is to born of the water and the spirit—it is baptism. In this the human spirit, not the flesh, changes in eternal ways. This was the answer, the light in his darkness that Nicodemus had been seeking, whether he knew it or not.

Secondary Preaching Theme

One of the most oft-quoted Bible verses is John 3:16, which speaks of God's love for us and how we will never perish and have eternal life if we believe in Jesus. God's love is open and available to all. God gave God's only Son to show us the magnitude of his love. This is the kind of love that is mutual and full of God's grace. God's grace sent Jesus into the world not to judge it but to save it, because salvation was the very mission of Jesus.

Salvation is being saved and delivered from sin through faith in Jesus Christ. Paul tells us in Romans 4:1-5 that we are justified (made righteous) by faith alone and not by any works. Being justified by faith is knowing your relationship with God. There is no room for us to boast because our justification is not about our work. Abraham was saved not because of what he went on to do but just because he believed God's word and promise. Period.

Psalm 121 is David's way of reassuring us that our faith in God is all we need as we travel through this life. No matter what life brings, we are to put our confidence in God and be under his protection and care.

Genesis 12:1-4a shows Abraham's faith through his obedience to God. Believing in God makes it easier to obey because we believe God will do what God said. Faith was revealed when Abraham waited for God's timing and not his own timing.

Responsive Reading

L: We are obedient for we believe and have hope in the Lord.

P: We have confidence that God will do what God promises.

L: Our hearts rejoice in God.

P: We praise God's holy name.

L: God's plans are firm and will stand the test of time.

P: God moves in the fullness of time and is never late or early.

L: To enter into God's kingdom is to be born again.

P: We must have an outward sign of an inward grace—a change of heart.

Benediction

Go in the peace of God knowing the light of God will be in all your dark places. Share peace, joy, and love in Christ's name. Amen.

March 19, 2017
Third Sunday of Lent

Exodus 17:1-7; Psalm 95; Romans 5:1-11; John 4:5-42

Gathering Prayer

Almighty God, from you comes the water of life, living water that quenches our thirst on this long journey. Our trust in you and our love for you show when we await your divine timing. May we cross over thresholds that encourage the teaching and learning of who you are and the love that abides in you. Help us to let go of our fears and worries and do your will. In Jesus's name. Amen.

Preaching Theme

It is daytime and Jesus traveled from Judea to Galilee through Samaria. In this story it is apparent that Jesus could have chosen to avoid the Samaritan people, but he intentionally travels through that place that many others in his day did avoid whenever possible. The Samaritan woman is an outsider, but not only she but also her whole community lacked power and position. Jesus meets the woman at Jacob's Well. Jesus meets her where she is and evangelizes her where she is located. Similarly today, how can we bring people to Christ and to Christianity if we are nowhere near the people who need Christ in their life? If we are not in their location, how can we meet them? Only by walking with them and alongside them can we find the best opportunity to fulfill our mission of reaching others and inviting them into the Christian community.

To walk with them is to be where they are and to be willing to really be with them. Just think of your life and the reason you learned to worship and glorify God. Wasn't it because someone was willing to meet you where you were to show you the way? Then you became a true worshipper by placing God at the top of your list each day and in every way. By being introduced to God, your heart was changed and you began to live a life of love and service as Christ lived. A true worshipper makes God first and gives thanks daily for all the blessings we have received, for all that God has done for us.

Secondary Preaching Themes

It is significant that Jesus stayed with the Samaritans for a while. "They asked him to stay with them" (John 4:40) or abide with them. That word *abide* is a powerful word. It evokes other times when Jesus talked about abiding in him even as he would abide with us. Jesus needs to be that close to people if they are going to acknowledge him as the Savior of the world. How could they call him their Savior if they were not close to him and if he were not close to them? Who can call Jesus the Savior of the world if they do not personally know him? Evangelism brings about true worshippers through breaking of social customs and, in the case of John 4, speaking to a woman at the well who was an outsider, a foreigner, and even despised in her own village. Yet Jesus spoke to her, was willing to drink from the same water vessel, and through all this introduced a living water the woman could never have found had Jesus not broken through the barriers to reach her. Only through personal communication could he tell her "everything [she's] done" (John 4:29). And through this many Samaritans became believers because they heard from Jesus when he stayed two more days with them.

Paul also brings true worshippers into a conversation regarding their beliefs and acceptance of Jesus Christ as their Savior in Romans 5:1-11. We are no longer enemies of God; therefore we are at peace with God. We are at peace as a result of the battle that was won through Jesus Christ who freed us from the power of sin. Jesus made it all possible so that we can pass through the door into a world where grace is a gift to all who believe.

Responsive Reading

L: Evangelism is commanded of us in the word of God.

P: We will go and reach out in extravagant love, baptizing people of all nations.

L: God's well never runs dry.

P: The water that gives everlasting life run from a never-ending source.

L: Jesus made it all possible.

P: Through our beliefs and acceptance of Jesus Christ we receive the greatest gift of all—grace.

Benediction

May the peace of God be with you as you flow like a living river. May you abide in others so they may abide in Jesus Christ our Savior. Amen.

March 26, 2017
Fourth Sunday of Lent

1 Samuel 16:1-13; Psalm 23; Ephesians 5:8-14; John 9:1-41

Gathering Prayer

Christ, who made the blind to see, expose us to your mercy and goodness whether or not we possess the gift of vision. Help us perceive the Holy Spirit, who stands ready to anoint us with peace and new life in every circumstance, including the deadliest. Invite us to see God with or without our eyes so that we may more clearly love others and discover how to become healers as you are. All these things we pray in your name. Amen.

Preaching Theme

Faith does not require a miracle but only to believe that Jesus is who he claims to be. The blind man in John 9:1-41 confuses many. The disciples assume at first that sin must have left him sightless. Yet Jesus explains that the man was born blind in order to reveal the light of God. After the man's sight is restored, Jews, Pharisees, and neighbors struggle to comprehend the healing. They ask again and again, "How can he now see?" His parents are also at a loss and politely deflect, "He's old enough. Ask him" (9:19, 23). Repeatedly harassed until he is eventually ousted from the synagogue, the newly seeing man can say only that since it's unheard of for a blind man to be healed, his healer must be from God.

Yet the newly seeing man does not recognize Jesus as the Son of Man when Jesus finds him. The healing is not enough. The seeing man must have his questions answered: "'Who is he [the Son of Man], sir? I want to believe in him.' Jesus said, 'You have seen him. In fact, he is the one speaking with you.' The man said, 'Lord, I believe.' And he worshipped Jesus" (vv. 36-38). Only when the newly seeing man receives answers to his questions does the opportunity to believe become clear. The Pharisees overhear the conversation and wonder if they have somehow overlooked the obvious about Jesus and misunderstood the true nature of sin. Jesus states that they have.

Also important to notice is that the author of John is tougher on the Jews than on Jesus, his disciples, and the man born blind. Even the parents are portrayed as lacking nerve. How can we preach about their negative reactions without generalizing their behavior to all Jewish people and without risking anti-Semitism? We must remember that Jesus of Nazareth was Jewish. We may also want to empathize with the resistance toward the formerly blind man. We, too, question the nature and authenticity of divine healing. For us who have never experienced miraculous healing, it is also important not to generalize the gift of sight given by Jesus. The blind man is healed, but the deeper insight is that faith is given to him and us by seeing and hearing the Son of Man when he calls. Faith does not require human vision or audition but believing in the answers of God.

Secondary Preaching Themes

Psalm 23 is a popular psalm and is often read at funeral services. Consider asking your congregation to memorize Psalm 23 for the sake of reminding them of God's deliverance now. Perhaps lead the community in mnemonic call and response of a passage like verse 6, "Yes, goodness and faithful love / will pursue me all the days of my life, / and I will live in the LORD's house / as long as I live." Committing the psalm to memory helps us contemplate how the mercy and goodness of God are ever moving toward us and maybe clearly seen if we look in retrospect for the activity of God in our lives as we live them.

In 1 Samuel 16:1-13 a new king must be selected for the Israelites, and God instructs Samuel not to be swayed by what "humans [see]. Humans see only what is visible to the eyes, but the LORD sees into the heart" (v. 7). Yet God, through Samuel, chooses David, who was "reddish brown, had beautiful eyes, and was good-looking" (v. 12). Sometimes the Bible appears to contradict itself. Consider another example from the New Testament. The details of the resurrection are different (Matt 28:2; Mark 16:5; Luke 24:4; John 20:12). Scriptural differences, however, do not dismantle the authority of the Bible but help us perceive how faith rests upon more than words. We believe in the God that the Bible only approximately conveys.

Prayer of Application

Into your healing hands we place our prayer, Son of Man. Awaken us to realize that we believe not because of miracles but by embracing your identity and receiving you as the Messiah. Answer our sincere and snide questions of faith and doubt, just as you did with the blind man, so that we may seek forgiveness from our sins and truly see who you are in order to enact holy transformation in the world today. All these things we pray to you, the invisible but healing and redeeming God. Amen.

Benediction

May Jesus speak to you generously, providing answers to your questions, and may the Holy Spirit provide clarity of purpose so that you might live into the light of God. Amen.

Like a Shepherd

Psalm 23

Meg Jenista

Imagine King David before he was king. Before Bathsheba and Uriah. Before he'd bested Saul with his tens of thousands. Even before he'd made a name for himself against Goliath. Imagine David before Samuel's visit, when the priest had run through all the older—more promising—sons, none of whom fit God's bill. Imagine David, just an afterthought in his father's lineup.

Samuel asked him, "Is that all of your boys?"

"There is still the youngest one…but he's out keeping the sheep" (1 Sam 16:11).

Imagine that David. Sitting on a flat rock under a scraggly tree on the outskirts of Bethlehem. Aiming his pebble-laden slingshot at a knot in the tree fifty paces away. Scanning the edges of the field, keeping an eye on that one sheep who keeps wandering away from the others. Imagine that David. An ordinary kid with an ordinary job.

Imagine him plucking out a few notes on a harp, singing the songs of his people. Imagine him setting new words to old tunes. Imagine him imagining the God of the universe through the lens of his experience in this paddock. With these sheep. Imagine the courage, the healthy pride, the chutzpah that would lead an ordinary kid with an ordinary job to sing a song:

"Like a shepherd, God will tend the flock; / he will gather lambs in his arms" (Isa 40:11).

An ordinary kid with an ordinary job telling the whole world that God…? Well, that God is—at least in this way—actually a lot like him.

Psalm 23 is a beloved text, popularly known well beyond the church or synagogue walls. It brings comfort at graveside, recognition even in the dementia unit at the nursing home. It assures believers in troubled times. It provides a metaphor that works on people's imaginations.

"The LORD is my shepherd" (v. 1). Even for a decidedly non-agrarian congregation we can see this, can't we? The still pool where there are no eddies to catch at the wool of the sheep, weighing them down, throwing them off balance into the water. We are thankful for pastures rather than rocky crags. We are grateful for the promise of green, inviting full and satisfied bellies. We can trust a shepherd like this. And because we trust God, we know God is guiding even when the path winds and twists, climbs and falls. The Shepherd who leads to good places is the shepherd who stays with us in the dark places too.

We do well to remember the nature of metaphor—that it is meant to lap at us, to tease and to play, to root down into our imaginations and nestle in there for the long haul. Its meaning, this metaphor, pulls from life experience. It tickles the imagination. And, as life experience changes, the metaphor is pliable enough to accommodate a new perspective.

And the metaphor is not the thing itself. God is not Shepherd by way of didactic, confining definition. God is Shepherd by way of images and resonance. The same way God is Great Physician and Mother Hen. The same way God is Father and Mighty Fortress.

Commentator James Mays says, "The Psalm's confession is based on the salvation history of the people and expressed the individual's participation in God's ongoing salvific history."[5]

And that "individual's participation in God's ongoing salvific history" crops up often enough in life to let us know—here is something that speaks to the way we are human. That we are wired to make sense of God by way of the world around us. That we are wired to see, in our own lives, a participation—however paltry or faltering—in God's ongoing salvific history. That the Eternal Word—that is, Jesus Christ—is spoken in our words and takes shape in our metaphors.

And this is, in fact, just the way it should be for a people who believe in the incarnation. For people who believe God is not a distant and disinterested spinner of the cosmos. For people who believe that, even in creation, God came and roosted over the waters. For people who believe God walked with Adam and Eve in the cool of the day. Who appears in dreams and burning bushes, in pillars of cloud by day and fire by night. For people who recite the mystery with John each Christmas, "In the beginning was the Word / and the Word was with God / and the Word was God" (John 1:1). Who really do believe that the baby swaddled up and lying in a manger was the "Word became flesh [who] made his home among us" (John 1:14). People who say of this God, "You are Alpha and Omega. You are A to Z and every possible letter combination in between." People who are so enamored of an incarnate God that we look for God, we search God out in ordinary places. People so mystified and tantalized by this God that we hunger to see, in our own lives, a participation—however paltry or faltering—in God's ongoing salvific history. That the Eternal Word—that is, Jesus Christ—is spoken in our words and takes shape in our metaphors.

Which is also, if you think about it, just as it should be for a people who not only believe in the incarnation but practice the sacraments. Ordinary things of this world, turned toward extraordinary purpose. That's what we say of the bread and of the cup. Ordinary things. It's what we say over the water poured into the baptismal font. Ordinary things. But turned toward extraordinary purpose. Used by God to extraordinary purpose.

Ordinary things used by God to extraordinary purpose. Ordinary things like an ordinary kid with an ordinary task on an ordinary Bethlehem hillside, who said, "The LORD is my shepherd." Like an ordinary mom or dad who, pacing the hall through the night with a teething infant, realizes "the LORD is my parent." Like a surgeon excising mutating cells with a scalpel who sees it clear as day, "The LORD is my physician." Each of us, ordinary in our own ways, with ordinary work, ordinary lives for the most part. But also, if we have the eyes to see it, a lot like that shepherd boy all those years ago. We, too, might craft words and shape metaphors for understanding that God is—at least in this small way—a lot like us.

The LORD is my mathematician.

The LORD is my social worker.
The LORD is my gardener.
The LORD is my counsel.
The LORD is my poet.
The LORD is my chief of staff.

We are made to seek insight into the character and person of God. Sometimes that insight might be closer than we think. Closer than our next breath, our next word, our next action. The LORD is my _____. Thanks be to God.

April 2, 2017
Fifth Sunday of Lent
Ezekiel 37:1-14; Psalm 130; Romans 8:6-11; John 11:1-45

Gathering Prayer

Thank you, O God, for your Spirit who dwells in us. The Holy Spirit, who raised Christ from the dead, rouses us from despair and hears our cries immediately. We hope and wait for you, O Lord, more than those who watch for the morning. And because your breath is our breath, we believe that one day we will come back to life like the dry bones of Ezekiel and of Mary and Martha's brother Lazarus. Thank you for the promise of life everlasting. Amen.

Preaching Theme

Believing in Jesus entails seeing the whole picture. Readers may recognize John 11:1-45 by the narrative about the resurrection of Lazarus and Jesus's weeping. The miraculous restoration of life to Lazarus happens only in John and only in seven verses. The crying of Jesus occurs in three Greek words [ἐδάκρυσεν ὁ Ἰησοῦς]. Yet what is perhaps not as obvious and equally striking is that two women—Mary and Martha—and their relationship with Jesus frame the entire passage. Lazarus succumbs to illness, and Jesus mourns and then resurrects him in Bethany, "the village of Mary and her sister Martha" (11:1). For the disciples, Jesus should not go there, since he was almost stoned in Judea. Thomas makes a wisecrack about ending up like Lazarus if they do. Yet the request of the women emboldens him anyway.

Jesus appears to hesitate as it takes him four days to arrive. Jewish custom requires burial at the time of death. Jewish belief indicates that the soul sticks around for only three days in the body. Lazarus is dead with a capital D. But Jesus's patient approach makes clear that death may be real but it is not final for those who believe in Jesus. He will awaken Lazarus so that the disciples may believe. When he does, that moment provides a glimpse into the mystery of the gospel (11:15).

In the final section of the passage, Jesus comes to the tomb of Lazarus and asks that the stone be moved away from its entrance. Martha dissuades him by mentioning that the body has a rotten stench. Jesus reminds her, "Didn't I tell you that if you believe, you will see God's glory?" (v. 40). The stone is removed. Upon thanking God the Father he cries out, "Lazarus, come out!" (v. 43). Lazarus appears wrapped like a mummy. They unbind him and let him go. The Jews that accompany Mary to the tomb are astounded by what they see and they believe. How does greater attention to Mary and Martha inform what we can preach about Jesus as the one who saves us from death and Lazarus as one who exemplifies the miraculous power of the gospel? How does belief in Jesus also compel us to pay attention to all of the characters in the story of God, and how does having a panoramic view of what God is doing in people of all kinds (male, female, siblings, the celibate, the dead, the afraid, and so forth) deepen our understanding of Christian faith? How do the human relationships portrayed in John 11:1-45 not only make the narrative vivid but help us imagine what it means to live into the promises of God today?

Secondary Preaching Themes

In Psalm 130 the psalmist waits for the Lord and finds hope in the words of God presumably as transmitted by believing communities, sacred texts, and divine revelation. Sometimes God does not disclose the way forward immediately or even soon. Notice that although the psalmist here cries out to God, God does not answer. Psalm 130 suggests with vibrancy the importance of developing patience for God's response, even as we plead for God to hear us.

Romans 8:6-11 reminds us that the Spirit of God dwells within followers of Christ. The Spirit of God brought back to life a dead God. If that kind of power radiates within us, then let us spark our imaginations and ignite our bodies to invite others to life, growing in spirituality and departing from sins of this world like violence, corruption, and unbridled consumerism.

Prayer of Application

Dear God, your Son, Jesus, along with Mary and Martha, help us see the gift of resurrection for Lazarus. Your unstoppable mercy, love, and power become three-dimensional for us as we consider the interaction of all three with you. Give us the insight to interpret not only that biblical story but also all the angles of our current world and its people as widely and deeply as you deem fit so that we might also detect where and how you are bringing new life to your children also today. All these things we pray in the name of God, the Father, Son, and Holy Spirit. Amen.

Benediction

May you never lose hope in the resurrecting love of God. Go with the confidence of those who believe in a living and returning Christ, and with the assurance of the Holy Spirit, who never forsakes us, even at the moment of death. May the life-giving hand of the Lord be upon you as you live and prosper in God's presence and love. Amen.

April 9, 2017
Palm and Passion Sunday

Isaiah 50:4-9a; Psalm 31:9-16; Philippians 2:5-11; Matthew 21:1-11 (or Passion Reading: Matthew 26:14–27:66)

Gathering Prayer

Son of Man, betrayed by your disciples, and seemingly abandoned by God, instill within us your courage and commitment to remain faithful even unto death. Grant us your mind. You, who never took advantage of equality with God, humble us never to take advantage of those born in the image of God. Enable us to trust you no matter how unfair our lives seem, so that we might graciously empower others to a faithfulness that does not falter even when everything crumbles.

Preaching Theme

Communion and prayer are practices of faith for when things get real. It is important to remember that the first Lord's Supper was shrouded by deception and abandonment by Jesus's closest disciples. Judas has already sold Jesus out for a song before the meal begins. Thirty pieces of silver are chump change for most shepherds. It's the price paid for a slave gored by an ox. But Judas is not the only betrayer seated at the table when it's time to begin. Jesus names Peter and all the disciples as deserters following the meal's conclusion (Matt 26:31). The sacrament is established at a table of deceit.

At Gethsemane, Jesus finds himself unsupported and alone as he prays. When Jesus goes looking for support from his disciples in the face of such unbearable silence, he finds them asleep. Jesus prays again and again in anguish, "Take this cup of suffering away from me. However—not what I want but what you want" (Matt 26:39). Yet God does not reply. When everyone awakes, Jesus is ambushed and arrested and led to his death. For Jesus, prayer is vital even when no one cares, when God seems silent, and when the end cannot be stopped.

Redemption still finds a way in spite of how little the Lord's Supper and the prayer of Jesus accomplish. Peter recognizes his own wrong and cries in remorse.

Judas returns the thirty pieces of silver and hangs himself. Yet the people do not relent in their betrayal by requesting the release of Barabbas and demanding crucifixion for the Messiah. Even Pilate excuses himself as he heeds the anxiety of his wife and the wishes of the crowd by finally washing his hands of the entire affair. Simon of Cyrene is bullied into carrying his cross. Passersby humiliate Jesus after he is raised to die by taunting him to save himself if he is actually God. Jesus frustratingly quotes from Psalm 22:1, "My God, my God, why have you left me?" (Matt 27:46). No one wants anything to do with Jesus, not even God the Father.

The dead rise from their graves after an earthquake to bear witness to the innocence and identity of Jesus. His opponents acknowledge, "This was certainly God's Son" (v. 54). Joseph of Arimathea, "a rich man" (v. 57), prepares Jesus's body for burial, sets it within a tomb he purchased, and rolls the stone to close the gravesite himself. Besides him, the only living ones who stick around and remain faithful until the end are Mary Magdalene and Mary, the mother of Jesus. Preaching the tragic overtones of the Last Supper and Gethsemane, as well as the gritty redemption that follows, strengthens hearers to grasp how resilient and real the sacrament and prayer are even when all seems hopeless and lost.

Secondary Preaching Themes

In Philippians 2:5-11, Paul recounts how Jesus doesn't revel in his equality with God. Even though Jesus has a name above every name and to which every knee should bend and tongue confess, Jesus of Nazareth maintains absolute humility during his ministry upon earth. Jesus is the Son of Man. Since we are called to have the same mind as Jesus, when we pursue justice, peace, and love with the oppressed, victimized, and vilified, we must also commit to a deep humility.

The psalmist knows utter despair in Psalm 31:9-16. Yet the psalmist trusts God despite feeling like one who is a dead and broken vessel. Piety may not cure depression, still anxiety, or wipe away our tears of mourning. Yet placing our future into God's hands does involve praying as the psalmist does by learning from the language and honesty of Psalm 31 and praying in concert with and through all of the other measures we adopt to stem our pain.

Prayer of Application

Jesus, whose Last Supper and final prayer with the disciples are shadowed by betrayal and the silence of God, help us also to recognize that you welcome the weight of sin and doubt in our world today at each celebration of communion and in every moment of supplication. By approaching your table in all circumstances and by praying to you honestly at all times, introduce us to experience your inexplicable but utterly real mercy in our lives. We pray fervently in your Holy Spirit. Amen.

Benediction

Hosanna! Let us welcome the shining face of the Jesus who has come to save and accept the guidance of his light into the most shadowy aspects of real life. May we align our minds with his and become humble witnesses to the Holy Spirit in the world. Let us listen for the echo of the Lord in all places. Amen.

April 13, 2017
Maundy Thursday

Exodus 12:1-4, 11-14; Psalm 116:1-2, 12-19; 1 Corinthians 11:23-26;
John 13:1-17, 31b-35

Bidding Prayer

(If the song is familiar to the congregation, you may substitute the first verse of "I Love the Lord" for each recitation of the psalm.)

We gather in God's presence for a service of remembrance. We remember Israel's story. A story of people crying out in slavery and set free. A story of people crying out in the wilderness and set down in the promised land. Of people crying out in exile, set into the very heart of God.

We love the Lord, for he heard our voice; he heard our cry for mercy.

We remember the story of Jesus who walked with the disciples, healed the sick, taught those who would listen. He heard the cries of the whole creation and made his home among us.

We love the Lord, for he heard our voice; he heard our cry for mercy.

We remember our own stories. Stories of overflowing joy and sorrowing tears. Stories of success and disappointment. Stories, always, of God's presence.

We love the Lord, for he heard our voice; he heard our cry for mercy.

In the name of the Father, the Son, and the Holy Spirit we pray. Amen.

Preaching Theme

Jesus is up to something. It is strange, even unseemly, that a teacher would serve so humbly. Based on the responses, it certainly made those involved rather uncomfortable. But here Jesus does what Jesus does. Jesus is inviting people to come, as they are, to encounter his grace. The exchange between Jesus and Peter in the first seventeen verses of John 13 holds up a mirror to our own spiritual condition. We might wonder: What was the nature of the relationship between Jesus and Peter? What tone of voice is used? What looks are exchanged? What do the onlookers think? Peter questions Jesus. Peter refuses Jesus. Peter ultimately accepts Jesus. When God seems up to something strange in our lives, we have questions too. When God seems to be saying, "Just go with it and I'll explain later," we might refuse God too. But when Jesus promises that we can be with him, that we might have a part in what God is doing in the world, we may find ourselves compelled, with Peter, to say, "Lord, not only my feet but also my hands and my head!" (v. 9). All of me, Lord! For your service!

Secondary Preaching Themes

Exodus 12 provides intricate detail for the celebration of the Passover. It is striking that God even makes consideration for those who cannot provide for themselves. If someone does not have enough to afford a lamb? Well, share. There is an expansiveness to the original Passover feast, one that ought to find parallel in our Christian celebrations of the Lord's Supper. At the table of grace, people who do not have enough find abundance from God and they share it with their neighbor.

First Corinthians 11, on either side of the Lectionary text, is an argument that has been used by the church to restrict or fence access to the table. There are dire warnings issued: "Those who eat the bread or drink the cup of the Lord inappropriately will be guilty of the Lord's body and blood" (v. 27). Further investigation in the text reveals that the people of Corinth were not sharing their meal with everyone. They were saving the best bits for the rich and influential. They were offering just the scraps and leftovers to the poor and less popular among them. Jesus, who welcomed a denier, a betrayer, and a whole bunch of cowards to his table, would certainly have something to say to those who are stingy around his table of grace.

Maundy Thursday is one of the most strangely named holidays on the church calendar. It is always worth stopping to explain the Latin origin. The name derives from the Latin phrase *mandatum novum*, translated "new commandment." Returning to John 13, we read Jesus's words, "I give you a new commandment: Love each other. Just as I have loved you, so you also must love each other. This is how everyone will know that you are my disciples, when you love each other" (vv. 34-35). The God of Hebrew Scripture ensures that all the people of Israel can participate in the grace of the Passover meal. Jesus plows through the disciples' resistance and uncertainty to offer them his love. Paul, in the epistle, admonishes the church for prejudice and pride-of-place at the table. In each text we find an application of the *mandatum novum*, love as Christ has loved.

Invitation to Foot Washing and/or Table

Jesus invites us to trust him as he takes our dusty, calloused feet in his hands.

We will participate in Christ's love.

Jesus invites us to come with open hands and a willing heart.

We will participate in Christ's love.

Jesus invites us to approach a table set by the one who knows our weakness the best and loves us the most.

We will participate in Christ's love.

Jesus invites us to make room at the table for others, without selfishness or pride.

We will participate in Christ's love.

April 14, 2017–Good Friday

Isaiah 52:13–53:12; Psalm 22; Hebrews 10:16-25; John 18:1–19:42

Gathering Prayer

Incarcerated Jesus, you knew they were looking for you. Denied Jesus, you entrusted your church to Peter who pretended three times as if you were a stranger. Beaten Jesus, you surrendered to Pilate and faced execution as your chosen people granted amnesty to a bandit. Crucified Jesus, you carried your cross alone. And yet before you took your last sip, your last breath, and spoke your final word, you in love gave your mother, Mary, a new son and your disciple a new mother. Entombed Jesus, executed Jesus, we thank you that in your death we find light to see all people as our family. Amen.

Preaching Theme

In the Gospel of John Jesus faces death alone, but his crucifixion unites the family of God. When Jesus says to his mother, "Woman, here is your son" (19:26), and to the disciple, "Here is your mother" (v. 27), he is not simply asking that they look after each other like relatives in the wake of his tragic death. He makes clear that faithfulness to him (which they both display by remaining steadfast at the foot of the cross until he gives up his spirit) means establishing a new family on earth as directed by God. Even the death of God does not stop the radical nature of God-given love. In fact the perishing Jesus empowers us today to stretch our arms widely, even if in an anguished manner as he did, so that we can embrace every neighbor as siblings, parents, and extended family, including those who have journeyed with us until the bitter end and those whom we would rather leave behind (15:12). Though the message may seem basic, how can we generalize Jesus's dying wish to Mary and the disciple into a wider imperative for our hearers to care for all others as family too? Especially with recent broadcasts of unimaginable religious and prejudiced violence, how does the final instruction from a dying God for an unrelated mother and son to become family to one another become a foundational approach for us as we decide how to respond to the slaughter of innocents? As we remember the sacrifice of the crucified Jesus on Good Friday, how does remembering his last mortal words of revelation to Mary and John bring into focus what following Christ entails and provide an ethic that heals in every circumstance, including grieving after the death of God?

Secondary Preaching Themes

In Hebrews 10:16-25, the Holy Spirit testifies to us that God will write God's laws upon our hearts and our sins will be forgiven and forgotten. We are also reminded that Jesus promises to remain faithful. *We* are reminded. The Spirit testifies to *us*. The gifts of Christian faith are experienced collectively. Therefore, the writer of Hebrews also stresses the importance of gathering together for worship. In a world where individualism, especially with regard to religious belief, is championed, the wisdom of Hebrews recommends a very different approach to devotion: shared reliance and pursuit of God.

In Matthew 27:46 and Mark 15:34 Jesus quotes from Psalm 22 on the cross— "My God, my God, why have you left me?" In John, his last words are, "It is completed" (19:30). The cry from Matthew and Mark also voices how we often feel. Knowing that Jesus felt abandoned even as we sometimes do and that Jesus died even as we all must die grounds the Christian faith within the harshest plains of reality. The emphatic statement of John also reassures us that we do not believe in fantasy. We pray to a God who receives our loudest frustrations and who remains in control, even in the midst of a barbaric and certain death. Imagine and embrace the vulnerability and the invincibility of Christ as you lead your congregation into the womb of Good Friday.

Prayer of Application

Father and Mother of all people, you instructed Mary and the beloved disciple to become family for one another as they watched your Son's final moments on the cross. Compel us also to love and take responsibility for one another as those who are related by your blood. So that we might tangibly live into your desires, crucified Jesus. All these things we pray in the gift of your Holy Spirit. Amen.

Benediction

Family of Christ, God is faithful even when evil encircles us. Do not become dismayed by the world's violence, even when God seems put to death by humanity. Depend upon the vitality of the Holy Spirit and do not tire of loving your enemies as brothers and sisters and fathers and mothers no matter how violent the world becomes. God will bring judgment, peace, and the renewal of all things. Amen.

April 16, 2017
Easter Sunday

Acts 10:34-43; Psalm 118:1-2, 14-24; Colossians 3:1-4; John 20:1-18

Call to Worship

L: Hurry! The sun is up. The tomb is empty.

P: Light breaks through. Joy comes in the morning!

L: Hurry! The tomb is empty. He is not here.

P: We come to see for ourselves—this emptiness that means new life.

L: Hurry! How long will you seek the living God in places of death?

P: He is not here. He has gone out before us!

L: Hurry! We have witnessed resurrection; life, where all was once decay; hope, where all was sorrow.

All: Hurry! Run to share the news. Hurry! We live again to tell the story.

Preaching Theme

There's so much running in the first part of this story! Following the marathon of Holy Week, we can easily fall into the breathless rhythm of John's narrative. Hurry! Come and see! It's finally here!

That momentum takes us right through the cave and hurries us out to the garden with Mary. As natural as it feels to let the Easter sermon center around her revelatory scene, I want to dwell for a moment on the unnamed disciple: the one whom Jesus loved and the one who beat Peter in the race to the tomb.

While many biblical scholars have speculated about this disciple's identity, the anonymity carries a measure of drama and mystique. I'm content to let the unnamed disciple remain unnamed and wonder, instead, what compels this character to run faster. He (or she?) reaches the tomb a few frantic paces ahead of Peter. What's the hurry? Maybe it's something about being unnamed...the designation of "other," which is pretty much the only thing we know about this friend of Jesus. Perhaps those whom the world has named Other—outsider, outcast, outlier, stranger, forgotten— perhaps they are always the first to arrive. They seek hope more urgently. They are the first to find that God is no longer to be found in the old places, in the old ways, but has risen to take on a new kind of embodiment for those that convention and tradition have rejected. Perhaps our congregations could hear in this reading a challenge: to hear the old story anew through the ears of the "other" and then seek new ways of reaching out to those on the fringes with the hope of resurrection.

Secondary Preaching Themes

An empty cave, in and of itself, is nothing to write home about. But emptiness, in the place of death, is big news. Drawing out that imagery, we could explore all the ways in which our context leads us to seek life in places of death. We may dwell in that which "once was" or might have been; we place our faith in fallible systems; and/or we attach too much value to things that aren't actually alive (like electronic devices...). Asking this question—How long will we seek life in places of death?—we could explore any of those cultural "narrows." Ultimately, it is human nature that we will cling to things that can't give us life. Easter is the reminder to shed the empty shells that weigh us down and embrace the emptiness itself. In that darkness, in that mystery, miracles happen. True story. (The song "Roll Away Your Stone," by Mumford & Sons, would be a great complement to this message. Some of the lyrics could even be drawn into the sermon itself.)

It would take a brave preacher to *not* preach the gospel story on Easter Sunday. But what if we were to hear Acts 10:34-43 in the context of the resurrection scene? Like a cinematic flash forward from the empty tomb, we go to the moment that Peter addresses the gathering at the home of Cornelius. This address points to Peter's revelation that God does not pick favorites. Peter, despite his Jewish context, has reached the epiphany that *even the Gentiles* can be included in this new thing God is doing among them. What journey led him from the first glimpse of the empty tomb to proclaiming such a radical truth to this little band of "church," gathered in a friend's home? That would be an interesting path to explore.

Words of Institution and Communion Prayer

Once, Jesus gathered the people he loved most, and he said, "Everything is about to change. So I'm going to give you something. That as often as you need to eat—as often as you hunger for righteousness—I will be with you, as long as you remember me. And as often as you need something to drink—as often as you thirst for justice and mercy—I will be with you. As long as you remember me." And so we do.

God of new life: Bless this bread to nourish our bodies, that we might feed all who hunger for you. Bless the cup that we share as a sign of our oneness in you, that we might be one with all the world. Draw us together in the grace of this table. And send us out, renewed in the hope of your love. Amen.

April 23, 2017

Acts 2:1-4a, 22-32; Psalm 16; 1 Peter 1:3-9; John 20:19-31

Gathering Prayer

Living God, gather us into this space, this time, this season. Send your spirit to move among us. Open our hearts and our minds, that we will not hear you from "behind closed doors" but from a place of deep desire and readiness. Renew our call to embody the good news, to speak resurrection in places of despair. We seek you, in the fullness of joy, and in the wholeness of community. Amen.

Call to Worship

L: This is the time to let go of fear and embrace hope.
P: This is the place to release our burdens and accept God's mercy.
L: This is the season to begin again and make things new.
P: These are the people who will remind us of God's grace.
L: The living Christ dwells among us, the promise of everlasting life.
All: The living Christ lives within us, the promise of boundless love.

Preaching Themes

Poor Thomas. Our watered-down Sunday school lessons make him the cautionary tale, the embodiment of "weak faith." Jesus was right there in front of him, and he needed more proof! What kind of disciple was he? Of course, a more mature reading of the story knows the answer to that: What kind of disciple was he? The regular kind. The human kind. The same kind as the rest of us. Of course he was doubtful. Aren't we all? Of course he needed something to see, touch, hear, taste, smell. Don't we all?

All believers, on occasion, need to hear a sermon on the important role of doubt in grown-up faith. We all need assurance that healthy skepticism only serves to refine our relationship with the holy; that "certain" belief is at best arrogant and at worst downright dangerous. A great passage from the novel *A Prayer for Owen Meany* might be useful in this context: "Mr. Merrill [their minister] was most appealing because he reassured us that doubt was the essence of faith, and not faith's opposite."[1]

But beyond the affirmation of our real life there's another layer of opportunity here. On any given day, I can get past my own doubts by recalling all the times I knew, for certain, the present faithfulness of God. I can count the blessings I've received at unexpected times; I can name the many people who embody love and mercy for me; I can cite the provision of God's abundance in creation, and at my own table.

But what about those who can't?

The story of Thomas makes me think not only of the value of doubt but of the relative ease of faith when one has love, and food, and shelter. The world is full of those who doubt God's existence not because their faith is weak but because they've rarely been loved, or fed, or gathered into the safety of community. Maybe your congregation has a certain population that will be near and dear to its own heart: the elderly and alone, the homeless, the mentally ill, the at-risk youth. This would be a good Sunday to highlight some of those mission/ministry areas and also hear the story of Jesus's appearance through the ears of those who might not have as many daily reminders of his constant loving presence.

Anyway you approach it, the message for the second Sunday of Easter does not have to be mere affirmation for those who believe but a challenge to embody the life-giving proof of resurrection for those who don't. In fact "Living Proof" would be a great title, hook, or image to carry through the whole service.

Secondary Preaching Themes

Using the same text, you could play up the image of the disciples gathering "behind closed doors." There's something powerful about that picture of Jesus's friends, hiding out at home in the aftermath of Jesus's death. Of course they were afraid. Of course they were terrorized. The people who had killed Jesus were certainly looking for them next. Into that fraught atmosphere arrives Jesus himself, and he "breathed on them" (John 20:22), so that they might receive the Holy Spirit. This would be a wonderful story to draw out a little more (taking some narrative liberties, of course). And it could lead to some challenging questions about the ways in which we might be "hiding out" in the safety of home (or church) when Jesus comes calling us out into the world.

There's a great line in 1 Peter 1:3-9: "Although you've never seen him, you love him" (v. 8). Peter says others can know and love Jesus through those who already love and know him. People we don't know can meet Jesus in and through us. We love others, and through us they come to love Jesus. How can we love people we've never met? And what does that kind of love teach us about the love of Christ?

April 30, 2017

Acts 2:1-4a, 36-41; Psalm 116: 1-4, 12-19; 1 Peter 1:17-23; Luke 24:13-35

Invocation

God of mystery, dwell within us and move among us. Draw us near to the wonder of Christ's love as we recognize it in our neighbor and forgive us when we fail to recognize it in a stranger. We seek your mercy, new every morning, as we serve those in need. Speak to us in unexpected voices as we worship together and as we move through our days. Call to us in unusual words and ways so that we will rise to respond. Move through us as in extraordinary and seemingly ordinary pathways that we might never be surprised to find you walking alongside us. Amen.

Preaching Theme

Two of the disciples are headed to Emmaus. Surely they were still reeling from the loss of Jesus, but something keeps them moving. As they walk along, Jesus falls into step next to them. "What are we talking about?" he wants to know. They respond: "Haven't you heard? Are you the only visitor to Jerusalem who is unaware of the things that have taken place?" In short, *"What rock have you been living under?"* ("Well, actually . . . ," begins Jesus.)

It is almost comical as the friends share a long account of Jesus's death and resurrection . . . with Jesus himself. Was he just letting them ramble on because he found it amusing? Or because he knew they wouldn't believe him if he tried? And for that matter, why didn't they recognize him?

Maybe the answer, though far less funny than Jesus making rock jokes, is simple: they were heartbroken.

The Pixar movie *Inside Out* gets into the head of Riley, an eleven-year-old girl whose family has just moved to San Francisco. While her whole life thus far has been mostly happy, she struggles with sadness at leaving her friends behind and adjusting to a new school, city, and hockey team. The main characters—the feelings inside Riley's head—work together to help her process all the change. Their biggest challenge turns out to be this: in the process of all that moving, the "Sadness" character touches some of Riley's old memories and finds that her touch turns them blue. In other words, once sadness starts to move around inside of you, it can color even your happiest memories.

In seasons of grief or just difficult transition, nothing looks or sounds as it should. We might find ourselves feeling lost and alone, and even those closest to us can't reach us. Change and loss can leave even the most familiar things unrecognizable. I'd venture that every person in the pews (or chairs) will be able to relate to this on some level.

So how does love transform sadness? What does resurrection mean when we are lost and hurting? What does it take to draw the brokenhearted back into fullness of life and hope?

In Riley's case, it had everything to do with the embrace of her parents and her place at the family dinner table. It seems like we could say the same for those disciples. He stayed with them, and they didn't know him. They sat together, but they could not see him. Then he broke the bread, and they said, "Of course that was him. Of course it was. Our very hearts were on fire, when he came around..."

Secondary Preaching Themes

The Emmaus Road story is also a lesson in *being prepared* to recognize the holy in everyone we meet, regardless of whether or not we were expecting to meet God in just that way. Stories of unexpected allies, strangers in need, or the formation of community in an unlikely setting would illustrate this truth well. Read Ann Patchett's book *Bel Canto* or watch the movie *The Way* to further explore the transformation that can take place when people are drawn together through tragedy or in the midst of chaos.

Psalm 116 presents an interesting tension: that of being free while also being a servant. Chris Tomlin's arrangement of "Amazing Grace/My Chains Are Gone" would be a good worship complement and point of reference. Using the images of becoming *unbound*—alongside the psalmist's use of servant language—could lead to some meaningful discussion about the things that bind us all. What "bindings" are harmful? (Addiction, other people's definitions of worth, material wealth, abusive relationships, and so forth). And, as the psalmist suggests, what ways of being "bound" might also give us life (community life, marriage, pro-reconciling movements, peace and justice work, and so on)? With these images in mind, we might lead people into a deeper understanding of servant leadership and how it might transform the church, the workplace, and the world.

Benediction

Wherever your week might take you, may you find that the Risen One walks alongside you. May you hear that voice of hope, comfort, and challenge in those you meet along the way; and may you be the voice of mercy to those who wait in your path. Go in peace, go with joy, and go with God's blessing. Amen.

May 7, 2017

Acts 2:42-47; Psalm 23; 1 Peter 2:19-25; John 10:1-10

Call to Worship

L: The good shepherd calls us in to find shelter.
P: The shepherd calls us out, to eat the green grass.
L: The shepherd calls us in to gather, to find warmth, to be protected.
P: The shepherd calls us out, to drink the cool water.
L: The shepherd carries us when we are sick or hurting.
P: And he puts us down to run free when we are well again.
L: We enter the gate as the shepherd calls us home to safety.
ALL: And we leave again as he sends us: from life in the fold to life for the world.

Preaching Theme

John 10:1-10 is already a sermon. We may struggle with John's mixing of metaphors (how can Jesus be the shepherd *and* the gate?) but even so, this text is rich in imagery that "preaches" all by itself.

Since the metaphors are a bit redundant, it may be wise to choose one and run with it. For instance: *The sheep know the sound of the shepherd's voice.* That's nice in a parable. But in actual, day-to-day life of discipleship, does it translate?

Every day, we are saturated with visual stimuli and with noise. It all adds up to voices. Voices everywhere: coming at us from billboards, through cell phones, in social media and the twenty-four-hour news cycle, from people in our lives (for better or worse), from our own internal self-talk, and from a thousand other sources that may or may not be telling the truth. And that may, or may not, be giving us life.

This is a good time to talk about authority. Of all the people in our lives, to whose voices do we give the most weight? Of all the sounds we hear each day, to which do we give our attention and energy? Of all the ways "the Shepherd" might speak to us, are we really prepared to hear that voice calling over and above the rest? Spiritual disciplines might not always get top billing in the sermon, but daily prayer, reading, writing, or mindfulness can certainly make us more receptive to that "voice," however it might reach us over the chaos.

Secondary Preaching Themes

Acts 2 presents an almost utopian view of life in the early church. The people lived together and shared everything. They worshipped together, they ate together, they lived simply. No one lacked for anything, and everybody got along. It sounds a lot like the first week of college dorm life. But check back in again around finals time, and you might hear a very different story! This passage lends itself to some thoughtful critique of culture: our fierce individualism, rampant consumerism, and era of (often self-imposed) isolation. The church should be asking hard questions about the ways in which Christians support and enable these systems.

The Twenty-Third Psalm can seem almost rote. It might be the only passage that many have memorized as children, and you can almost bet on it being part of the funeral. What if we were to reframe this popular verse in a way that would allow people to hear it in a fresh way? This rewrite, "Psalm 23-and-a-half" includes the original text, but draws it out to place the "What is" alongside the "what could be." It could be used as a prayer, a transitional text, or part of the sermon:

> The Lord is my shepherd,
> whether I like it or not.
> I shall not want.
> Except for a bigger house, a nicer car, a slimmer waistline;
> a newer device, a little more power;
> and to always, always, every day, be right about everything.
> He makes me lie down in green pastures
> as the world grays with concrete
> and browns with toxic fumes
> and bleeds with violence and rage.
> He leads me beside still waters
> even though I pull away, and make a run for the choppy sea
> of my own thoughts, complaints, and addictions.
> He restores my soul.
> from its own self-inflicted wounds.
> He leads me in right paths for his name's sake . . .
> For his name's sake,
> even as I celebrate with my own signature.
> Even though I walk through the darkest valley, I fear no evil;
> even as I log on, tune in, and worship at
> the altar of fearful story
> that we call news.
> For you are with me;
> even as the world spins into chaos, crippled by the hatred of other,
> Your rod and your staff—they comfort me.
> They tell me a better story,
> And call me back to your side.

You prepare a table before me in the presence of my enemies
And ask only that I sit and dine with them.
You anoint my head with oil;
And call me to live a life worthy of this benediction.
My cup overflows
With sorrow, with remorse,
With gratitude.
Because for all my selfish, wandering, fearful, and faithless ways,
I know that
Goodness and mercy shall follow me all the days of my life,
Even now. Even on the worst day, the worst week, the worst moment
Of the created, human world.
And I shall dwell in the house of the Lord my whole life long,
Singing a new song,
And telling the Shepherd's story
Into the darkness.

With Glad and Generous Hearts

Acts 2:42-47

William Willimon

I want to talk to you today about an act of worship that you might have not thought of as worship—the offering.

In the early church, the offering consisted of the people's gifts of bread and wine for the holy meal. After the service, leftovers were taken (in the words of Justin Martyr) to "the orphans and the widows, and those who are needy because of sickness or other cause, and the captives, and the strangers who sojourn amongst us."[1]

I've heard people say that, in the age of plastic money, the charge card, computerized banking, and revolving credit, couldn't the church find a more efficient, less-intrusive way of collecting its due?

People, please pay attention as the plate is being passed down the pew, as people place their gifts in it. Pay attention as the Jones family comes forward when the offering is received, bringing the loaf of bread and the pitcher of wine for Holy Communion, for something very important is happening here. The offering is a significant statement of faith.

The persistent danger of our Sunday worship, the sacrilege against which we must be eternally vigilant, is the tendency to divorce Sunday worship from daily life. It is the danger that all our hymns, our anthems, our soft organ voluntaries, our poetic preachers, our beautiful churches might somehow conspire to turn worship into an event that has nothing to do with everyday life. Unless there is some link between our worship of God and junior's spilt cereal at breakfast, the boring routine at the office, the monthly collection of bills, the cancer that will not heal, then our worship is not only irrelevant to human need but also unfaithful to the gospel of Jesus Christ.

Never think that Sunday worship is mostly a "spiritual" affair, as we like to use the word *spiritual*. Christianity is an incarnational faith, meaning "in the body." Jesus is here as a visible, tangible sign that God could truly love us only by coming "in the body," by becoming incarnate in a Jewish carpenter's son from Nazareth. There may be religions where practice is confined to what you do in some holy place, hermetically sealed from the stress and strain of everyday life. There may be religions in which things like political debate, bodily health, material well-being, and physical needs are irrelevant. Christianity is not one of those religions. Here is a Lord who comes to us, not to take us out of this world but to give us a way to live in this world.

Every time we receive the offering, we are giving visible, tangible expression to the materiality of the Christian faith. We are lifting up ordinary things like bread, wine, and money and saying that because of the life, teachings, death, and resurrection of Jesus, these ordinary things take on new significance for us. In his ministry Jesus was always taking the everyday stuff of life—seeds, birds, flowers, coins, lepers, children—lifting them up, setting them in the context of God's kingdom, and thereby giving them redemptive significance. After meeting Jesus, after listening to his stories, you can't walk by a hungry person, or lift up a loaf of bread, or pick a flower, or gaze into the eyes of a child quite the same way as you did before meeting him. Ours is an incarnational faith.

How many times have you felt that your minister was forever urging you to "get out there and do something" but never gave you anything specific to do?

Now, in the offering, it is your chance to do something. The offering is, in a way, the test of our worship. Is this service only a time to sing a few hymns, think a few lofty thoughts, feel a few warm fuzzies, and go home to a big meal? Or is this a time to "put our money where our mouth is"? Remember how Jesus noted that our hearts are usually where our money is and vice versa.

The offering isn't an unwarranted intrusion; it is the acid test of what we are about. It yokes our faith to our jobs, our daily cares and concerns, what we shall eat, what we wear, where we live, how we vote. We shouldn't apologize or be embarrassed by this act of worship, for it is an act that typifies the peculiar Christian stance toward the world, a stance typified by the person of Jesus himself.

"I think that the main business of the church is to stick to saving souls and stay out of politics."

"I think preachers should stick with theology and avoid controversial subjects like economic, business, or political matters."

"What a person gives or doesn't give is his or her own business."

"I'm tired of churches talking about nothing but money, money, money. They should be concerned with more spiritual matters."

How we wish it were so!

In a former church of mine, we were in a board meeting debating how to conduct the church's annual stewardship campaign. The discussion was becoming heated, and emotions were beginning to boil. One member said, "I get so tired of all this talk about money. I hope that we can get this kind of thing out of the way and get on to more important church business—like religion!"

I responded, "Well, what is our business? Perhaps all this talk about money is not a religious matter. But don't you find it interesting that we have been meeting all year, discussing all manner of church business without even a mild argument? Yet, when we discuss money, suddenly everyone gets very heated. I have a feeling that we may at last be discussing *the* really big concern for most of us."

The offering is the link, the necessary connection between our intentions and our deeds, our spiritual impulses and our materialistic commitments. The offering reminds us that Christian worship is an ethical affair. A Christian does in church on Sunday that which he or she does Monday through Saturday in the world, namely, to offer one's life to God. Our actions, our gifts, our deeds are our offering, our way of giving back to the God who has so graciously given to us.

Did you hear this note in our first lesson today, Acts 2:42-47? Acts says that, after Easter, at the end of Pentecost the church gathered on a weekly basis in order to devote "themselves to the apostles' teaching, to the community, to their shared meals, and to their prayers" (v. 42). That's us on Sunday, just like the first apostles at worship. Isn't that what we do on Sunday?

Yet the scripture continues: "All the believers were united and shared everything. They would sell pieces of property and possessions and distribute the proceeds to everyone who needed them" (vv. 44-45).

Note the link between worship in the church and their lives in the world, the way they linked economics to liturgics, Sunday to Monday.

You want to know the test of our worship? It's how "together" we are as the church; it's if our worship of God in church is able to produce "glad and generous hearts" so that we are concerned about those in need.

It's how well we are able not just to listen to the word or to sing the hymns but to show forth our gladness and generosity in offering ourselves and our gifts to God. Amen.

May 14, 2017

Acts 7:55-60; Psalm 31:1-5, 15-16; 1 Peter 2:2-10; John 14:1-14

___

Gathering Prayer

God, you are the first and you are the last. As we gather together, remind us that you are bigger than our temporary circumstances. Reveal to us your love that extends beyond the uncertainty of our future. May our time together be an opportunity to rest in the eternal love that you have for us. Amen.

Preaching Theme

The disciples were incredibly confused. According to the narrative of John's Gospel starting with chapter 12, Jesus entered triumphantly into Jerusalem, only to immediately tell his disciples that the mountaintop experience was a mirage and he was going to die a brutal death. Then he takes the role of a slave and washes their feet, indicating that they are called to do the same. Finally, he rebukes the favored disciple Peter in front of them all by saying that Peter will reject him three times. The heads of the disciples must have been spinning. In an effort to comfort them and bring them peace, Jesus speaks to them the language of love in John 14:1-14. Christians have often been guilty of using Jesus's words "I am the way, the truth, and the life. No one comes to the Father except through me" (v. 6) as a weapon that creates insiders and outsiders. Instead of giving the disciples a sense of who is in and who is out, Jesus was attempting to speak the deep language of love. In ancient Jewish marriage customs, a man would bargain a price with a father for the privilege of marrying his daughter. Once the terms were settled, the groom would enter a waiting period of twelve months when he would return to his father's house to prepare a room for his new bride. Jesus's disciples would have recognized that he was speaking to them using the language of marriage and marital love. He was telling them that they do not need to worry and that he is everything they need. Jesus was expressing that his commitment to the disciples was forever and that his love would extend beyond the uncertain future. Jesus's words come to us today and force us to consider if we will trust the deep love of Jesus to carry us through an uncertain future.

Secondary Preaching Themes

It jumps out that the three other lectionary passages all make mention of a stone. In 1 Peter 2, the people of God are referred to as "living stones" and Jesus is the "capstone." In Psalm 31, God is a "rock" of protection and a "fortress" that provides salvation. In Acts 7, the men of the Sanhedrin stone Stephen to his death. The contrast is stark: stones have the power to preserve and save life or the power to destroy life. Even though the stones destroyed Stephen's mortal life, he received the love and trusted the promises of Jesus in John 14, which carried him through a painful present and an uncertain future. Stephen's blood became part of the living stones that God used to build the church.

Psalm 31 is a beautiful prayer of trusting God despite a painful present and an uncertain future. In Acts 7, Stephen becomes a living example of this prayer. The psalmist cries to God, asking to be delivered from enemies and rescued from harm. In Stephen's case, the prayer was not answered as you might expect in his most dire moment. However, the prayer remained on his lips to the bitter end as he prayed, "Lord Jesus, accept my life!" (v. 59) and then, "Lord, don't hold this sin against them!" (v. 60) with his final breaths. Stephen provides a powerful witness that the worst thing is never the last thing and that true faith in the deliverance of God extends beyond the pain and suffering of this life.

Congregational Prayer (Based on Psalm 31)

God, we take refuge in you. Do not let us be put to shame.
Rescue us by your righteousness. Hear us when we cry out to you.
Deliver us quickly from the net that has been set to trap us.
Be the rock that protects us and the fortress that saves us.
God of faithfulness, we entrust our spirits into your hands.
Our future is in your hands. Shine your face upon us.
And save us by your faithful love.
Amen.

Benediction

My friends, as you leave this place, remember this:

We may not be able to escape the plans of our enemies, but neither will we be able to escape the love of God.

We may not be able to escape pain and suffering, but we can always take refuge in the one who is our rock and our fortress.

We may not know what the future holds, but we do know the one who holds the future.

Go in peace knowing that the eternal love of God is with you.

May 21, 2017

Acts 17:22-31; Psalm 66:8-20; 1 Peter 3:13-22; John 14:15-21

Gathering Prayer

God, we come together today to remember what you have done in the past, to consider where you are at work in the present, and to anticipate the arrival of your kingdom in the future. History has revealed that you keep your promises and give life. Give to us today a word that we need to hear using a language we can understand. Speak, Lord, for your servants are listening. Amen.

Preaching Theme

The situation Paul encountered in Acts 17 has a lot of parallels to living in the twenty-first century. While Christianity may still be the primary religion in the West, the number of people who profess to be Christian is dramatically declining so that those who claim to be Christian are feeling increasingly like outsiders. In addition, idol worship is still present, though in different forms. Imagine that thousands of years in the future archeologists who know little about us are digging through the remnants of our current society. What would they conclude about their findings? Might they conclude that in almost every single household the people would gather around a flat-screen box for a time of worship? Or would they assume that every city had a temple to the god of the golden arches, the bell, and the cute red-headed girl? Without getting too dramatic, it is safe to conclude that our society is becoming increasingly secular. Paul's interactions with the people of Athens provide critical insights into how those who profess Jesus as Lord should engage an increasingly secular society. Our task is to reveal Christ by telling the story of God using a language that people can understand. Paul quotes one of their own poets to help convey God's truth. As Christians living in the twenty-first century, we are called to engage our society using a language people can understand. We need to familiarize ourselves with the work of current poets, authors, artists, and entertainers so that we know how to speak the language of our society. And we also need to be excellent at telling stories. We must be able to narrate salvation history in a way that captures the attention of people and meets them where they are.

Secondary Preaching Themes

A nice parallel exists between Paul's evangelism to the people of Athens and the exhortations of 1 Peter 3. The author of 1 Peter encourages the faithful by saying, "Whenever anyone asks you to speak of your hope, be ready to defend it. Yet do this with respectful humility, maintaining a good conscience. Act in this way so that those who malign your good lifestyle in Christ may be ashamed when they slander you" (1 Pet 3:15b-16). Paul was ready to speak of his hope in a way that was respectfully humble to the people of Athens. First Peter 3 then provides the posture for how we should approach telling the story of God. We should be prepared at any moment to reveal Christ by telling the story of God using a language people can understand, and we should do it with a posture of respectful humility.

A theme that exists in the John 14 reading, as well as the 1 Peter 3 reading, is the presence and promise of the Holy Spirit. Jesus knew that his time was short with his disciples and he wanted to bring them peace. He promised that after he was gone, his Father would send a companion, who would be "the Spirit of Truth." The Spirit of God will be present with us as we attempt to reveal Christ by telling the story of God using a language that people can understand.

Psalm 66 provides another example of sharing the story of God. In verse 16, the psalmist says, "Come close and listen, all you who honor God; I will tell you what God has done for me." The psalmist then goes on to declare that God has listened to his or her prayers and did not withhold love. Notice that the psalmist uses poetry to communicate the story of God.

Prayer of Repentance

God, we confess that we have often failed to represent you well. We have become so consumed with our own stories that there have been many times we have neglected to tell yours. We have been ignorant of moments that provide opportunities to share the reason for the hope that we have. In your mercy, O God, hear our prayers. Free us for joyful obedience, that we may be empowered to engage our culture and reveal Christ by the way that we live our lives. Send your Holy Spirit to fill us and give us the ability to share the good news of your salvation. Amen.

Benediction

My friends, as you leave this place, you are entering a world filled with people who need to hear a good story. Remember that you are a minister who is called to tell the story of God and shine the light of Christ into the darkness using the gifts and the talents that you already have. Know that you are not alone. The Spirit of God goes ahead of you and will be present with you. In the name of the Father, the Son, and the Holy Spirit we pray. Amen.

May 25, 2017–Ascension Day

Acts 1:1-11; Psalm 47; Ephesians 1:15-23; Luke 24:44-53

Gathering Prayer

God, we gather to remember the day your Son, Jesus, ascended bodily into heaven. Just as the disciples must have felt overwhelmed and alone after the ascension, we confess that we often feel overwhelmed and alone. Send us the gift of your promised Spirit, that we may be empowered to be your witnesses wherever we go. Amen.

Preaching Theme

The disciples had been through a lot. They witnessed the rapid rise and fall of Jesus's ministry. They thought they had given everything to follow Jesus, but when it all came crashing down and in his greatest moment of need, they all either abandoned him or flat-out denied they had anything to do with him. After Jesus's death, they essentially returned to their old way of life. And then the rumors started. Jesus was alive, risen from the dead. With a mixture of doubt, disbelief, and faint hope, they met the risen Christ. But then the disciples must have been confused when Jesus gives them a curious instruction: "He ordered them not to leave Jerusalem but to wait for what the Father had promised" (Acts 1:4). But Jerusalem was the place haunted by the memory of their failure to stay with Jesus. Rather than avoiding Jerusalem, Jesus invites his disciples to remain in their place of failure until they received the promises of God. Like the disciples, we are quick to run away from our places of failure. We want to distance ourselves from those relationships and situations where we have failed. The primary text on this Ascension Day may be inviting us to consider those times in our life when we have failed. What if our failures could be a new opportunity to receive the promises of God?

Secondary Preaching Themes

The Gospel reading from Luke 24 tells the same story as Acts 1, though in a different way. However, the same central message of remaining in their place of failure until they receive the promises of God is found in Luke 24:49: "Look, I'm sending to you what my Father promised, but you are to stay in the city until you have been furnished with heavenly power."

The contrast of the disciples' reaction to the ascension of Christ is interesting to note. In Acts 1 the disciples are seemingly stunned and stand there looking into the sky. Finally, two men in white robes come to them and question why they are looking into heaven and offer a word of hope. Later the disciples are in an upper room with the doors locked out of fear right before Pentecost happens. In Luke 24:52, the text says that they returned to Jerusalem "overwhelmed with joy." It can be important to point out that either reaction to a call of returning to our places of failure is appropriate. For some people, it can be a great release and a moment of joy to think that enough time has passed that they can now revisit their places of failure with new eyes and understanding. For others, it can grip them with fear and stun them. Either way, the promise of God is that the Holy Spirit will meet us in our places of failure and work to bring redemption.

The Apostle Paul provides an interesting example of the theme that God calls us to return to our place of failure to receive the power and promises of God. Paul's failure included the persecution of the early church. In a remarkable turn of events, Paul awkwardly returns to his place of failure with the apostles in Jerusalem seeking their forgiveness and instruction (see Acts 9). Paul received the power of God and became zealous for spreading the good news all over the known world.

Prayer of Repentance

Forgiving God, as we are aware of your presence, we set aside time to revisit our failures. We confess that we have failed to be an obedient people. We have not loved you with our whole hearts. We have failed by what we have done and what we have left undone. In the silence of this moment, we remember and confess those times in our life when we have failed.

[Offer period of silence for silent reflection and prayer.]

God, we wait for the gift of your promised Spirit to come and redeem our failures. Use our failure and our weakness to build your kingdom. May your redeeming love rise out of the ashes of our brokenness and failure. Amen.

Benediction

My friends, receive the good news: Christ has risen from the depths of the dead and into heaven where he is seated at the right hand of God the Father. In light of that good news, we no longer need to be defined by our failures. Instead, through the power of God's Spirit, our failures can be redeemed and used for good. As you leave this place, leave with overwhelming joy and the expectation to receive the power of God's Spirit.

May 28, 2017

Acts 1:6-14; Psalm 68:1-10, 32-35; 1 Peter 4:12-14; John 17:1-11

Gathering Prayer

God, we give you thanks for drawing all of us together to this exact time and space. Pour out your Holy Spirit on us that we may be able to display the unity that exists between you and your Son, Jesus. Make us a witness to the world that you are one and that we are one with you. Do not allow conflict and differences to tear us apart, but unify us in a way that not even death could destroy. Amen.

Preaching Theme

John 17 gives a fascinating and intimate look into the prayer life of Jesus. It begins with Jesus's awareness that his time is limited and that he is nearing the completion of the mission for his life. The deep and eternal connection of the Son with the Father is revealed with Jesus's request to be glorified with the glory Jesus shared with the Father before the creation of the world (John 17:5). The intimate focus of the prayer quickly shifts to the disciples and those with whom Jesus has shared life. Jesus prays for their safety, but ultimately asks that "they will be one" just as Jesus and the Father are one (John 17:11). It now seems prophetic that participation in the life of God should lead to unity and oneness. Through globalization and dramatic advancements in transportation and communication technology, the world has become a small place and humans have been thrust into relationship with one another on a global scale. While many examples exist about the beauty of connections that transcend barriers, our world is also marked by deep division. The prayer of Jesus in John 17 is a reminder that the purpose of the church is to reveal God in the world by being one, the coming together of a people around the story of one who loved so much he was willing to be broken and poured out for the life of the world.

Secondary Preaching Themes

The call to oneness is clearly seen in the charge of Jesus to his disciples in Acts 1:8: "You will receive power when the Holy Spirit has come upon you, and you will be my witnesses in Jerusalem, in all Judea and Samaria, and to the end of the earth."

In Acts 2 we learn that people from all over the world could be found in Jerusalem and the good news about Jesus is for them as well as the disciples who were the first witnesses. The good news of Jesus is for everyone, and it is the work of the Holy Spirit to draw all people together. The rest of the book of Acts is a story about the early church's attempt to grip this new reality where everyone is called to be one with God. One way to narrate the history of the church is as a constant struggle to realize that we are all brothers and sisters with the same God as our Father.

The text from 1 Peter 4 provides words of comfort for those who are suffering because of their association with Christ. As a people who are called to model and live into the oneness of God, there should be an expectation that suffering and persecution will come. The call to follow after Jesus is a call to deny oneself, pick up a cross, and be willing to die (Matt 16:24). The path that Jesus blazed is a path of loving God by loving others, and greater love has no one than this: to lay down one's life for one's friends (John 15:13). If we are more willing to lay down our lives so that others will live, we will cut against the grain of a world where people are willing to take lives in a vain attempt to preserve their own.

Responsive Reading (Based on Psalm 45)

Let God rise up, and let the enemies of God scatter.

Sing praise to the Lord.

Let the wicked perish before God like wax melting before a fire.

Sing praise to the Lord.

Let the righteous be glad and celebrate before God.

Sing praise to the Lord.

God is the father of orphans and the defender of widows.

Sing praise to the Lord.

God settles the lonely in their homes, and he sets the prisoners free.

Sing praise to the Lord.

Recognize the majesty of God.

Sing praise to the Lord.

God is the one who gives strength and power to God's people.

Sing praise to the Lord!

Benediction

As you leave this place and head into the world, may you recognize the presence of God in everyone you meet. May you create peace everywhere you go. And may you reveal the oneness of God by the unity you demonstrate with all that has life. Amen.

Abundant Joy

John 17:6-19

Karoline Lewis

Prayer. We know we need to do it. We try to do it. We hope to do it. Maybe we schedule it. Because otherwise, there tend to be more pressing matters. Like everything, actually. And sometimes prayer is more pressing than others. We like it.

If we are honest, prayer is hard. I mean, you are supposed to be having a conversation. With God, of course. But still. It's a different kind of conversation, right? I don't know about you, but mine tend more on the monologue side than the dialogue side when it comes to prayer. I don't hear much from the other party. Do you? The answers are delayed. Cryptic. Puzzling. Unanswered. And sometimes prayer is kind of disappointing. Or weird. Like I'm just sitting around hearing myself talk. Sometimes obligatory comments and observations. Other times desperate petitions. Really desperate.

Which is why this passage from John kind of rocks my world. How often do you get to hear a prayer, about you, for you, on behalf of you, that's this long? What is it about overhearing a prayer for *you*?

Because, here's the thing. Once someone finds out you are remotely religious, you get to be the pray-er. I always dreaded that. When people first knew that I was in seminary, or on internship, or had graduated from seminary, there was the inevitable, "Is there a pastor in the house?" You *always* get asked to pray. And I always wanted to say, "Listen, people. Do you not know that there was no such class at seminary? That I never had a course in spontaneous prayer?"

Yet there is something quite touching, quite poignant, that this text from John is the designated Gospel reading by the Revised Common Lectionary for the last Sunday of Easter. It is Jesus's prayer for his disciples that his disciples actually get to hear. No "stay here while I go pray." No, "WAKE UP PEOPLE!" (CLAP, CLAP, CLAP.) But a foot washing, comforting words of accompaniment, the promise of the Paraclete, and now, a prayer, for them, for their present and for their future. I imagine this like when I was a child, when the bedtime prayers were me listening to my mother because I could not voice them yet. Or those times when someone prays for you because you cannot find the words to do it on your own.

You have to wonder what the disciples thought at this point. What did they actually hear? Perhaps there was some serious selective hearing going on? Did they hear words of encouragement? Of protection? Of unity? Or, did they hear that they would be hated? That they don't belong to the world? That they would be abandoned? That Jesus is really leaving? For real. For good. In the words of Emilie Townes, were they scrambling to rearrange the deck chairs on their *Titanic* theology? Or just oblivious, in denial, devastated? Or maybe, quite possibly, implausibly, sadly, it was all of the above.

I wonder if they overlooked the one line so easily passed over, so quickly taken for granted, or so unbelievable that it must be, has to be, ignored. I wonder if they could have heard joy. "I say these things while I'm in the world so that they can share completely in my joy" (John 17:13). When can you hear joy? And when can't you?

Can we only hear joy when we know joy or we are in a moment of joy? Or, do we need to hear, can we hear joy, or know joy when we least feel it and expect it? When it seems the most absent? When it seems the most impossible?

There is something extraordinarily and devastatingly elusive about joy. It is not mere happiness, and how much we pretend that it is. That if we could just be happy, optimistic, that there's an expected equivalence. That joy would then just automatically follow.

But really, true joy? When do we know it? When do we feel it? Even the usual times and places that we name as moments of joy are not necessarily so—the birth of your first child, a graduation, the remission of cancer. Is joy possible, ever again, when depression has taken its hold, when the only hope seems like the sacrifice of yourself, when giving in to who you are means giving up on who you thought you should be?

And, how can there be joy when a betrayal is at hand? When injustice will most certainly occur? When death is inevitable? Seriously, Jesus, what in the world (literally) is going on? In the words of a guy I know named Nicodemus, "How can these things be?"

The joy of which Jesus speaks—the joy that might become complete, made full, provided fully in every single one of Jesus's believers—is a perfect, passive verb. That is, we have been filled with the joy of Jesus. But that joy is forever in our present.

In other words, this is abundant joy. Like everything else that is abundant from Jesus: the best wine, acceptance in the midst of ample rejection, nourishment when it seems that most will be left hungry, light when there is utter darkness, sight when there has been only blindness, a new community when one has been thrown out of the fold, life when there is absolute and certain and most certainly death. I find it interesting that the Greek words for *grace* and *joy* are only two degrees of separation. Two letters to be exact. As if perhaps grace and joy are related. As if joy is the feeling of grace upon grace.

I think it's remarkable that Jesus in this prayer holds both together at the same time. The inevitability of sorrow, the expectation of suffering, the knowledge of betrayal with the absolute certainty of joy. The joy of which Jesus speaks breaks into every abandonment, every hopelessness, every pain.

Maybe this is the true meaning of the resurrection. How we can imagine the joy of resurrection carrying forward beyond Easter. Because, let's face it, it's no easier to live out the resurrection than it is to live into the reality of the incarnation. No wonder one church sign I saw after Easter said, "Open between Easter and Christmas."

On the brink of Pentecost, when the church year leaves the resurrection behind, we desperately need to know that resurrection joy is not only possible beyond Easter but actually possible for our present. That resurrection is not some future life, with mansions, and rooms, and crowns…insert heavenly wishes here…but where joy really and truly breaks into the present. Is that what Jesus wants us to hear on this last Sunday of the Easter season? Wait, that's the Lectionary committee talking. But, could this be what Jesus wants us to hear before he is arrested, put on trial, and crucified? That joy is here and possible, now and in what is to come?

Is this what it means to be human, that when we hold together the divine and the human, God and the Word made flesh, we are somehow, miraculously, insanely, holding together every hard thing that it means to be human with the joy that our being human can mean?

So, as we move into the season of Pentecost, or, in other words, the long season of life, this is what we need to remember and hear. This is what we need to know and realize. That on this last Sunday of Easter, joy is there when you don't feel it. Joy can be heard when your ears can't hear it. Joy is visible when you cover your eyes from seeing the pain.

Such is the Christian life, is it not?

Whatever story you need to imagine that captures both at the same time, the aching of humanity with the profound joy of faith, this is the heart of Jesus's prayer. Where do you go?

Here's where I went. Here's when it happened to me, one Mother's Day not so long ago. My oldest son wakes up, comes into the kitchen where I am unloading the dishwasher—what else would a mother be doing on Mother's Day, after all? Yet, it was a day like any other, because every morning in our house is a check on how much he has grown—overnight, of course. And, every morning, I humor him. I shrink a little. "Sig, you have totally grown! You are almost as tall as I am! How did this happen?" He so desperately wants to be taller than me. And he can't stand it when I wear heels.

But that morning, and I will never forget it, he really was taller. He really was. No more feigning. No more abating. No more saying, "You are so close, Sig!" And it's a lot easier to shrink than it is to rise on your tippy toes so as to avoid and avert the truth.

And it was Mother's Day. And I want him to be taller and the twelve-year-old he wanted to be. And to know that it's okay that his move into maturity necessitates being measured by the height of his mother. And every single morning, I feel him slipping away. Every single morning is that crazy moment, that crisis moment, that excruciating moment of both joy and grief, when you want them to grow and to go, and yet every single part of you, every single place inside you, every single pore of your being, wants them to stay and to want you and to need you.

And in that very moment, for me, was a flashback to when I first became a mother, nine weeks before I was supposed to, at least three to four pounds of a baby before what was expected, and four weeks before the birth classes for which I registered were to begin. Before I got to that chapter in the book, for heaven's sake. In the midst of the joy of having my first child was an early labor, a premature birth, a significant stay in the NICU, months of therapy, $1,200-a-month shots to keep him from getting the common cold...I'll just stop there.

Is this what Jesus meant? That you could realize joy and heartache twelve years apart? That you could know joy and pain in one event? That you could experience joy and sadness in one single second?

Yes, I think this is what Jesus meant. I think this is what Jesus had in mind. I trust that Jesus knew, really knew, that to be human is to know the abundance of joy and the pain of letting go. In the very same second.

Yet, what joy it is to know that Jesus lived what that means.

June 4, 2017
Pentecost Sunday

Acts 2:1-21; Psalm 104:24-34, 35b; 1 Corinthians 12:3b-13; John 20:19-23

Gathering Prayer

God of peace, we your people gather in expectation: fearful, anxious, curious, and excited. Come into our midst, calm our restless hearts, and help us hear your call to go into the world. Help us remember your saving words, your words of good news, and your words of restoration for us and for the world. May your peaceful presence make us a forgiven and forgiving people, through Christ our Lord. Amen.

Preaching Theme

The Holy Spirit is active, empowering, courage giving, and the great remembrancer. We tend to focus our Pentecost celebration on the dramatic aspects of the Acts narrative: tongues, flames, and crowds. What if this year we focused on the fruit of the coming of the Spirit? On the power to forgive, on the gifts given to all for the common good, and on our unity as God's people? I think focusing on these things will help our congregations connect with their own longings, with how the Holy Spirit is at work in their hearts and life, and with how each of us is truly an agent of the Spirit in the world.

At the cornerstone of our power to be proclaimers of forgiveness is the reality of our oneness in Christ. Our oneness is the first fruit of our salvation, and it connects us to a tapestry of fellow forgiven folks, a people who know what it is like to begin again. We come from different places, speak different languages, live from different cultures, and live into our forgiveness in different ways. The Spirit's coming reminds us of our commonality as God's creation and on the power of our unity in the midst of our differences. Our different gifts, through our different stories, provide fertile ground for the common good for all creation, a reminder of the creative promise of God at the beginning of time.

Pentecost reminds us to claim our particular gifts and to allow ourselves to be propelled by the baptized community to become agents of God's forgiving message knowing that it is too good to withhold from anyone.

Secondary Preaching Themes

The Spirit's coming has cosmic consequences. People from all places and all times gathered on that day according to Acts. People, from all walks of life, live around us, work with us, and might even enter our spaces of worship. The Spirit sent to us by God is hovering, ready to unleash its saving power on all people. We often think of the work of the Spirit in such limited and restrictive ways. Yet the narratives for this day speak of bounty, awe, wonder, and limitless hope! Thinking in this way should inspire our congregations to look around and see the ways that the Holy Spirit is active around them so that they can shine a light on that work and join the Spirit's work in their neighborhoods, places of work, and homes.

The reading from John 20 tells us that if we withhold forgiveness it will be withheld. What might this mean for us today? Forgiveness is not an easy task. It requires time, effort, and a recalibration of the relationship. A slow forgiveness might in the end be a healthier one. What are some of the ways that our congregations can model the slow yet deliberate work of forgiveness and reconciliation?

Responsive Reading (Based on 1 Corinthians 12)

There are different spiritual gifts **but the same Spirit.**

There are different ministries **but the same Lord.**

There are different activities **but the same God who produces all of them in everyone.**

Each person is given the Spirit's demonstration **for the common good.**

Wisdom **is given by the Spirit.**

Knowledge **is given by the Spirit.**

Faith **is given by the Spirit.**

Gift of healing **is given by the Spirit.**

Performance of miracles **is given by the Spirit.**

Gift of prophecy **is given by the Spirit.**

Ability to tell spirits apart **is given by the Spirit.**

Different kinds of tongues **are given by the Spirit.**

Interpretation of tongues **is given by the Spirit.**

All these things are produced by the one and same Spirit, **who gives to each of us!**

Benediction

May the God who sent us the Spirit,

Who gave us the call to forgiveness,

Who made us one people, gifted for the common good,

Be with you as you go into the world in grace and peace!

In the name of the Father, Son, and Holy Spirit we pray. Amen.

June 11, 2017
Trinity Sunday

Genesis 1:1–2:4a; Psalm 8; 2 Corinthians 13:11-13; Matthew 28:16-20

Gathering Prayer

Creator God, you continue to make order of the world, to enter the chaos of our existence and to remind us that all you have made is indeed "very good." May we remember your call to be agents of your goodness, of your creative power, and of your restorative presence. May we remember your call for us to go into the world and through our loving lives, compel others to follow in the way of your Son, Jesus, in whose name we pray. Amen.

Preaching Theme

The Corinthian Christians were wondering about their witness. In the midst of everyday life, of the struggles of living the way of Jesus, of the ways that the world around us pushes us to respond differently, how are we doing?

It is difficult to self-assess, to take stock, to evaluate how we are doing in our discipleship. This requires an awareness of what the Holy Spirit is doing in our hearts and lives and how that work is bubbling up as we live our lives each day. It also requires attention to those people around us who have been empowered by the Holy Spirit to guide us in our way of discipleship.

Paul reminds the Corinthians to "put things in order" (2 Cor 13:11). To model God's work at the beginning of time by entering the chaos of their lives and the lives of others so as to be agents of order, encouragement, harmony, and peace. I would say that living in these ways might just be the most important sign of our work of discipleship, a key way that we as followers of Jesus live into our call to compel others, by our loving behavior, to become followers of Jesus.

If we are to be effective in our work of discipleship, we must be willing to help one another grow in love. To shine a light on how we can love better, reconcile with one another, and be encouraged. This is especially important in a culture that seems set on tearing others down, on stirring chaos, and on living in harmony only with those who agree with us.

Secondary Preaching Themes

Discipleship is a buzzword that so many of us struggle to define. What would it look like for us to teach what Jesus commanded? I think we might begin by engaging in a shared journey through the life of Jesus, studying what he commanded, the fruit of his activity on earth, and the key themes of his teaching. I imagine that engaging in this quick survey will begin to give a more concrete picture of the life of disciple-ship, a more objective measure to how we are doing, and will empower us to be more faithful in our work. Always remembering that doubts will still be present and that the re-creative work is never finished.

Jesus is with us always. He is with us as we live our daily lives, with us as we doubt, and with us as we take stock of our lives. Jesus is with us as we engage others and as we engage creation. Jesus is with us calling us back, reminding us that we are indeed created in God's image and part of the created order. Our journey with Jesus will indeed guide us all the way through the fulfillment of God's kingdom. Living in this way should be a reminder to stay humble, be encouraged, and to persist in God's loving work.

Prayer of Repentance

God, you have called us to compel others to follow your way by our practice of love, to be agents of your peace, to live in harmony with one another, and to be agents of order in the world. We confess that often we have failed to live in your ways by not modeling your way of love. Instead we have stirred strife, started arguments with our neighbors, and cre-ated chaos in our lives and in the lives of others. Restore us, O God, transform us through our doubts, and renew our commitment to new life. We claim our renewed hearts and our renewed lives and look forward to our common creative, restorative, and loving work in the world, through Christ our Lord. Amen.

Responsive Reading (Based on Psalm 8)

Lord, our Lord: **how majestic**

is your name throughout the earth!

You laid a strong foundation to protect us from our enemies,

Lord, our Lord: **how majestic**

is your name throughout the earth!

When I look up at your skies,

at what your fingers made—

the moon and the stars

that you set firmly in place—

I wonder what are we that you think of us?

What are we that you pay attention to us?

Lord, our Lord: **how majestic**

is your name throughout the earth!

You've made us slightly less than divine,

crowned us with glory and grandeur.

Lord, our Lord: **how majestic**

is your name throughout the earth!

You've call us to be faithful stewards of all creation,

all sheep and all cattle,

the wild animals too,

the birds in the sky,

the fish of the ocean,

everything that travels the pathways of the sea.

Lord, our Lord: **how majestic**

is your name throughout the earth!

June 18, 2017

Genesis 18:1-15 (21:1-7); Psalm 100; Romans 5:1-8; Matthew 9:35–10:8 (9-23)

Gathering Prayer

God, again and again you call us to a journey; a journey where good news is shared, where new people are encountered, where our plans are changed. Help us be attentive to your invitation, to be courageous, to pay attention, and to celebrate your work in us and through us. Help us see your presence when difficulties come, when plans change, and when we have to find a new way. May the people we meet, the strangers we host, and the companions we travel with become a sign and symbol of your saving promise. In the name of Jesus, who sends us on the way. Amen.

Preaching Theme

The story of faith such as we find in Genesis 18 constantly messes with our modern sensitivities. The idea of opening our doors to complete strangers and trusting them to have a message from the Lord seems naïve, irresponsible, and misplaced. We tend to think of ourselves as self-sufficient; all we need is our own take on things, our opinions, our perspective, our own hearing of God. Strangers are met with suspicion, lack of trust, and at times fear. If they tell us that they have a "word from God," most of us would think they are delusional or just arrogant.

Again and again God sends people. Unexpected people, empowered people, strange people to bring good news. Often the outsiders have a much better take on what God is up to than we do. Coming from the outside seems to bring clarity if we are willing to hear, to provide hospitality, and to respond.

I wonder what the folks around us would tell us of what God is doing. What would they say about our life together, our worship, service, and our witness?

We tend to think of ourselves as the ones who are sent, and we are at times. But I think Genesis invites us to open ourselves up to the possibility that there are folks sent to us and that those who might seem like strangers, might just be messengers from the Lord. Let's pay attention, for their coming might just be the continued fulfillment of God's promise to us.

Secondary Preaching Themes

A sent people, an apostolic people, are a people who must be willing to deal with the struggles of the journey we call faith. Our walk of discipleship with its twists, turns, and trials forms us into a holy people. Each step of the way, even when we do not realize it, shapes us into a more mature and effective community of the baptized. We indeed feel weak, weary, and worn from the difficulties of living the way of Jesus. At those times we are invited to reflect on Christ, who died for us, because God loved us that much. In our trials we are participating in the way of Jesus as we grow in grace and truth.

Imagine if at every baptismal service we would claim for this newly baptized person their gifts as kingdom bearers! We would tell their parents, them, and the congregation to go "heal the sick, raise the dead, cleanse those with skin diseases, and throw out demons" (Matt 10:8). I think this might just make some take pause and wonder if they really feel called to the waters of baptism. It might make some parents wait till another day to bring their children forward. Most of all it might just birth revival. It might be the reminder that all of us need as God's people that our call is not to sit in sanctuaries, hear a good sermon, and hear songs, but that we are a sent and empowered people to bring forth God's kingdom in visible ways.

Congregational Prayer

God of surprise,
strange visitor,
bearer of unlikely news,
and re-namer:

Open our eyes to your presence.
To the ways that you are at work around us,
especially to the way that our neighbors, co-workers,
and the people we bump into in our daily life
might have a word from you.

Calm down our anxieties and fears.
Help us tune our ears,
sharpen our eyes,
and silence our mouths
so that we can be space-makers for your visitations.

We ask you these things in the name of one
who is sent and sender,
Jesus, the anointed one. Amen.

Benediction

May the one who sends us into the world

to heal, resurrect, cleanse, and exorcise,

fill you, use you, and send you,

with the blessing of God,

creator, sustainer, and redeemer. Amen.

June 25, 2017

Genesis 21:8-21; Jeremiah 20:7-13; Romans 6:1b-11; Matthew 10:24-39

Gathering Prayer

God, through your Son, Jesus Christ, you remind us again and again that to follow is to struggle, to be harassed, to be misunderstood, to carry the cross, and to be willing to die to ourselves. Give us the strength to carry on, to recognize your presence in the midst of trials, and to welcome the new life that you promise to us and to all people, through Christ, our Lord. Amen.

Preaching Theme

It's hard to think that the way of love taught by Jesus would be a source of conflict. Yet again and again Jesus reminds us that indeed it is. In fact Jesus's own life, his healing, reconciling, and hanging out with outcast and sinners, ended up in his death. Most of us sit in our sanctuaries on Sundays safe and sound. We hear the stories of Jesus, his teaching, and his actions, and we smile and feel good about ourselves. We go about our lives, and most people around us claim Christianity as their religion.

For me the question this week is: Are we loving radically enough?

Loving the unlovable in our society can indeed be radical and controversial. Being agents of healing, of reconciliation, of light (especially to those in power) might also stir the pot and thus be rather dangerous. What if for a season of our life together as congregations we measured our effectiveness in kingdom work by how much harassment we suffered, how much trouble we got into, how much life we lost?

This week is an invitation to take seriously the call of Jesus to love God and neighbor with abandon, to recognize that our call to discipleship is not a call to being a majority, a call to power and control, a call to privilege and arrogance, but a call to denial, a call to love radically even unto death, a call to allow our coming alongside the least to become our resurrection.

Secondary Preaching Themes

Romans 6:1-11 reminds us again that discipleship is about death. This time, though, it is reframed in a way that places the emphasis on Christ. Here we have an opportunity to reframe the conversation with our congregations from an emphasis on individual sacrifice to our communal work as the body of Christ. If we are to die to sin, we must remind one another of the story of Jesus, we must call one another to accountability, and we must claim again and again our new life in Christ Jesus. In fact here in Romans we are reminded that death is the only way to new life. In a culture that is death averse, this conversation could become a much-welcomed message. Dying to sin is a daily practice of loving ourselves enough to choose love, connection, and restoration for ourselves, our neighbors, and all of creation.

No matter what happens in our lives, God remembers us! The story of Hagar and Ishmael reminds us that it is easy for us to find ourselves drowning in our difficult circumstances. Shame, guilt, and disorientation keep us from seeing beyond where we are. If we pay attention, we might just hear God's voice reminding us of the promise that we are not forgotten, that life is before us. Recognizing God's voice changes our perception and we begin to see possibility, potential, and new life where death once lived.

Responsive Reading (Based on Jeremiah 20:7-13)

Life is at times a struggle; God seems far and death near.

Let us be encouraged by praying:

God, you are near in our despair.

Lord, you enticed me, and I was taken in.

You were too strong for me, and you prevailed.

Now I'm laughed at all the time;

everyone mocks me.

God, you are near in our despair.

Every time I open my mouth, I cry out

and say, "Violence and destruction!"

The Lord's word has brought me

nothing but insult and injury, constantly.

I thought, I'll forget him;

I'll no longer speak in his name.

But there's an intense fire in my heart,

trapped in my bones.

I'm drained trying to contain it;

I'm unable to do it.

God, you are near in our despair.

I hear many whispering—

"Panic Lurks Everywhere!—

proclaim, yes, let's proclaim it ourselves!"

All my friends are waiting for me to stumble:

"Perhaps he can be enticed.

Then we'll prevail against him

and get our revenge on him!"

God, you are near in our despair.

But the LORD is with me like a strong defender.

Therefore, my oppressors

will stumble and not prevail.

They will be disgraced by their own failures.

Their dishonor will never be forgotten.

The LORD of heavenly forces tests the righteous

and discerns the heart and the mind.

Let me see your retribution upon them,

for I have committed my case to you.

God, you are near in our despair.

God, you are near in our despair;

now we:

Sing to you, we praise you

for you have rescued us

from the clutches of the evildoers.

A Whisper, A Shout

Matthew 10:26-27

William Willimon

Therefore, don't be afraid of those people because nothing is hidden that won't be revealed, and nothing secret that won't be brought out into the open. What I say to you in the darkness, tell in the light; and what you hear whispered, announce from the rooftops. (Matt 10:26-27)

I try to teach preaching at the divinity school. "Every sermon ought to be based upon a biblical text," I tell seminarians. "Get a text, try to figure out what it says, then preach it."

But as a preacher, and for would-be teachers of preachers, I'll let you in on something: I wish I could figure out not only *what* a text says but also *how* a text says what it says. How you say something can be as important as what you say. How you say a thing can be the thing that is said. The medium is the message, and all that.

Trouble is, we can't know how Jesus said what he said. We've got the words, fixed, lying there on a page. But you know that the meaning of words is more than that. *How* you say something becomes that which is said.

In so many biblical passages I wish I knew how Jesus said what he said. Did he have a smile in his voice? "You filter out an ant but swallow a camel" (Matt 23:24). Surely he did not say that as they speak in the law court. "Whereas the party of the first part hath alleged that the party of the second part has strained a gnat and..."

When were his nostrils flared, the pitch of his voice raised? "You are like whitewashed tombs. They look beautiful on the outside. But inside they are full of dead bones and all kinds of filth" (Matt 23:27). That had to be a shout.

I expect he said softly, "Neither do I condemn you. Go, and from now on, don't sin anymore" (John 8:11).

I know this for sure. Sometimes Jesus shouted. Sometimes he whispered. His was the sort of truth that required modulation. He wanted people to hear him. He had to talk loud enough and clear enough so that they heard. But there is that truth that must be delivered with care, now needing a shout, then wanting a whisper.

"Nothing is hidden that won't be exposed," he said. "Nor is anything concealed that won't be made known" (Luke 8:17). The whisper will become a shout. That which he told them in conversation along the road must become that which is proclaimed from a housetop. The truth must be uncovered. But how?

"You are the Christ, the Son of the living God!" (Matt 16:16) exclaimed Simon Peter one day along the road. Grand moment of revelation, great shout of recognition.

Jesus said to him in a whisper, "'Happy are you, Simon son of Jonah, because no human has shown this to you. Rather my Father who is in heaven has shown you.' . . . Then he ordered the disciples not to tell anybody that he was the Christ" (vv. 17, 20). A shout becomes the whisper.

A friend of mine (I'll call him Steve) was a Methodist preacher. He told us about boarding a plane on the West Coast heading for home. He settled into his seat and was joined by a man, well dressed in a conservative suit. Steve, knowing how it can be to be trapped on a long flight next to some intrusive chatterbox, immediately opened a book, stuck his nose in it, and prepared for a solitary flight.

He noticed that the man next to him pulled out a Bible, a pen, and paper, and began taking notes.

Oh, great! thought Steve to himself. *A long flight and I'm next to some kind of religious nut. If he finds out I'm a Methodist minister, I'm dead. I'll keep my eyes on my book and maybe he won't discover me.*

The man next to Steve hardly looked up. An hour into the flight, he was still hard at work taking notes from his Bible. Out of the corner of his eye, Steve checked him out. He didn't look like a nut. Looked normal. Why was a normal-looking person like that studying the Bible? Meals were served. Steve glanced at the man. He ate, still reading the Bible!

"I, er, notice that you are reading the Bible," Steve finally said, his curiosity getting the best of him.

"Yes," said the man, who returned to his meal and his Bible.

"I found that interesting," said Steve.

"Do you?" said the man, who returned to his work.

"I found that interesting because I enjoy reading the Bible. You seem to be studying it very intently. Why?"

"I'm a Sunday school teacher. Adult class. I'm working on my lesson for tomorrow," the man replied, with a touch of aggravation.

"Really? Well, I read the Bible too. I'm a Methodist minister myself," said Steve.

"Good for you," said the man, who resumed his work.

Steve later commented, "Now, that's evangelism. That's how it ought to be done. Let's be absorbed in the faith until others beg to know what holds our attention."

No one grabbed him by the lapel saying, "Let me tell you about Jesus." Sometimes a whisper is more dramatic than a shout.

She entered the hospital room. Kathy (not her real name) had just gotten a very tough diagnosis. Kathy sat in bed, a box of Kleenex beside her, and she was crying.

"Kathy, I had to come as soon as I heard," she said. "I'm so sorry," she said as she moved toward the bed to embrace her.

"How can you stand there, Sunday after Sunday and talk so piously about the goodness and love of God? Here I am, mother with two children. This is your loving God?"

And for two hours she just sat there in silence with Kathy. After two hours, Kathy said, "I think now, I can go on." That's a whisper. A whisper can be more noticed than a shout.

And what you have heard in the dark, go out and tell in the light. And what Jesus has whispered to you in church, you are to shout from the rooftops.

We don't do much shouting in this church. In some churches, they shout. We're too...dignified for that sort of thing here. I preached out in a big church in California. You know California.

"Brother," the host preacher said to me (that's how he addressed me, "brother"), "Brother, don't worry about letting the Spirit use you today. We have an excellent medical auxiliary."

"Medical auxiliary, what's that?" I asked.

"Trained women who handle people who get so caught up in the Spirit during the service that they might hurt themselves if we didn't have somebody to catch them," he said. "We've also got a cooldown robe for you after you finish preaching."

A cooldown robe? That's preaching with a shout!

Most of my preaching is that of a whisper. I don't want to make a big show of it. The days of the "pulpit princes" with their eloquence and elocution are gone. I'm too humble for that sort of thing.

"I'd rather see a sermon than hear one," as we say. "Don't wear my religion on my sleeve. Don't believe in making a big show of it," we say.

Yet Jesus commands us: "What I say to you in the darkness, tell in the light; and what you hear whispered, announce from the rooftops" (Matt 10:27).

At this year's Annual Conference, when all of us Methodists huddle together for a week of conviviality, we were just having ourselves a wonderful time. Sitting, listening to reports, going over last year's business, singing a hymn every now and then. Rumors were that we had some controversial issues to come before us, but they were unfounded. Just sailing along...until the last day of conference.

"Bishop," he said, "I've got a resolution to put before the body."

What's he *standing up for?* we wanted to know. We were just doing fine, on our way to adjournment. Why doesn't he just sit down and stay quiet?

"Bishop, estimates are that American troops have killed at least 3,500 civilians while performing operations in Afghanistan, mostly children. Bishop, we cannot sit by without some response on the part of our church to this sort of suffering and..."

There are some people who've got to shout what they heard whispered.

It is fine for the shout to become the humble whisper. But Jesus says it is even more blessed when the secret truth, whispered to the heart, erupts into a shout.

Her beloved daughter had been killed by a horrible criminal who lived only three doors down the street from them. Brutally beaten and worse. Left by the road to bleed to death.

They caught him. Had enough evidence on him to hang him right there. Convicted, easily. On the day of the sentencing she at last broke her silence, appeared before a bank of microphones and cameras, and said, "This has been a terrible, terrible blow to our family. I hope no mother must ever go through what I have. When I learned that he was the one who had done this, I wanted him to die as horribly as my little girl was murdered. But we're Christians. We are trying, we are praying, for the goodness of heart to forgive. I don't want this man to die. What would that do? I want him to live, to be made to see the truth, to repent, to be forgiven, and to work to make sure no one ever again does what he did. That's what we believe Jesus would want us to do."

> *. . . nothing is hidden that won't be revealed, and nothing secret that won't be brought out into the open. What I say to you in the darkness, tell in the light; and what you hear whispered, announce from the rooftops.*

July 2, 2017

Genesis 22:1-14; Psalm 89:1-4, 15-18; Romans 6:12-23; Matthew 10:40-42

Preaching Theme

The church cannot be all things to all people. And yet... the temptation to over-program and under-preach marks a constant presence in the lives of leaders. We want to offer a group, an activity, a connection point for every person at every age and stage of life. *And yet*... when it comes to proclaiming the gospel, we try to say as much as we can without really saying anything, without edging into that hot-button issue that we fear might fracture the congregation.

This brief passage from Matthew may seem like a surface message about personal sacrifice: about the ways in which our faith, and our personal relationships, deepen the most when we are willing to put self aside. It would be easy to preach—with very little preparation—all the ways that giving up some of "self" and stuff leads to more meaningful connection with family, community, and world. Get the folks home in time for the first inning.

However, this passage offers a more challenging route for the preacher who wants to question the congregation's boundaries of welcome. If a community's commitment to inclusion means avoiding tough topics, then this passage poses some difficult questions. Jesus exposes the tension between the passive welcome of "something for everybody..." and the hard work of giving people what they truly need. Prophets need to be welcomed as prophets and recognized as such; the needy and vulnerable need to be served with kindness and compassion and with the meeting of practical needs.

The church can't just fling wide the doors and expect for lives to be changed and communities transformed. The hard work of discipleship is getting to know our neighbors and meeting their deepest needs with our greatest gifts. The church can't do that without addressing some of the contentious issues that may be off-putting to some members. But sometimes losing a bit of ourselves makes room for love and life to grow. This text invites the reader to question what we might be willing to give up—*as individuals, and as community*—in order to truly embody the gospel, beyond just forming a knitting circle or a car club or a softball team or a dinner group or...

Take that where you will. Meanwhile, remember that Jesus talks of "sending" and "receiving" because this gospel message was literally being delivered by hand—before e-mail and texting, before the Pony Express. Those who receive the messenger will receive the one who sent it: Jesus himself. And those who receive Christ will receive the very presence of God. These days we don't rely on wandering pilgrims to bring us our mail. But we do, in so many ways, rely on strangers to challenge and shape our understanding of God's grace.

Secondary Preaching Theme

Genesis 22:8-21

Religious extremism is everywhere—from the horrors of terrorism in the Middle East to smaller-scale attacks in our own backyard. In that climate, the story of Abraham and the almost-sacrifice of Isaac appears as a lesson in what not to do—the very embodiment of all the worst things that religion can lead to. No amount of exegetical historical/cultural context placement can clean this one up: Abraham was about to kill his kid, and it was all God's idea.

However, God ultimately intervenes. Abraham is not the model parent or human in this text—he rarely is. In fact, the whole of Genesis is about people failing, falling short, and misunderstanding what is being asked of them. The overarching theme is of God's goodness, mercy, and faithfulness. The highly fallible person quotient is a constant throughout the narrative, if only to highlight how good God is in spite of people's unworthiness. So rather than dwell in the wheres and whys and what-not-to-dos of this text, the preacher could instead focus on the high point of this story: that God does not require human sacrifice, or any kind of bloodshed, for the grace and love that's freely given to all.

If the sanctuary has media capabilities, this would be an excellent story to explore through fine art renderings. From Rembrandt to more contemporary works, countless artists have interpreted this story. What do the images say about how sacrifice and atonement were viewed in each artist's time, place, and culture? That alone could be a rich discussion. Although, if there will be children in worship, it's a discussion that might be better saved for adult Bible study.

Prayer of Thanksgiving

God of mercy, you demand no sacrifice but ask only generosity. Teach us to be generous with our gifts, our time, and our spirit of grace, as you have shown goodness to your people through all of time. We lift up these offerings—not out of obligation, but out of gratitude and love. Bless them for the work of the good news in our community and world. Amen.

July 9, 2017

Genesis 24:34-38, 42-49, 58-67; Psalm 145:8-14; Romans 7:15-25a;
Matthew 11:16-19, 25-30

Call to Worship

L: For the gift of loving family,
P: We give you thanks, O Lord.
L: For the grace of gathered community,
P: We give you thanks, O Lord.
L: For the journey of following Jesus,
P: Give us courage, O Lord.
L: For the daily work of compassion,
All: Lord send your Spirit to guide us. Amen.

Prayers of the People

God of the Sabbath, you have given us the gift of time. And while you have promised us that there is a time for everything, we feel there is never enough. Forgive us when we fall into a pace that drains and depletes us; when we rush to make enough, do enough, be enough . . . even though, by your grace, we are enough, just being born of your image. Help us rest in the peace of your life; grant us the patience and the discipline to be present with those we love. Nourished in the goodness of those relationships, may we find the strength we need to be good neighbors and caring disciples. Teach us to walk in the way of Jesus—the way that restores, renews, and never weighs heavy—so that we might move freely as your Spirit sends us. Amen.

Preaching Theme

"Are you tired? Worn out? Burned out on religion? Come to me. Get away with me and you'll recover your life. I'll show you how to take a real rest. Walk with me and work with me—watch how I do it. Learn the unforced rhythms of grace. I won't lay anything heavy or ill-fitting on you. Keep company with me and you'll learn to live freely and lightly."[1]

That is Eugene Peterson's paraphrase of this text from *The Message*. "Recover your life!" What a welcome invitation, and one that many folks sitting in the congregation desperately need to hear. Many (preacher included) are guilty of worshipping at what Barbara Brown Taylor calls the "Altars of Busyness" on a fairly regular basis. Not only do we forget how to slow down and breathe, we often forget why we should.

But Jesus does not just call the work-worn and care-worn into a day of rest. He calls those who have been burdened by the rigid demands of strict religious creed to come away with him where the air is lighter and faith is a life-giving thing again. He promises to teach the "unforced rhythms of grace."

Understanding what religious "freedom" would have looked like in Jesus's time might help frame what this means for us today. Jesus did not mean to abolish the Law. Rather, Jesus's message was that love of God and other was at least as important as upholding the law—if not more so. While the Law was important, it was never meant to become more urgent than the needs of neighbor or the pressing demands of relationship.

Ultimately Jesus doesn't just offer freedom "from" confining religious code; it is a freedom "for" something. We are called to rest so that our bodies will be free for the work of serving others; we are called to free our spirits of constraint so that we'll be free to love generously and extend mercy.

The promise that all who follow Jesus will "recover your life" will mean one thing to the addict and another to the recently unemployed; it will mean one thing to the poor and homeless and something else entirely to the frazzled suburban parent. This passage extends challenge on the one hand and comfort on the other. And for all, a much-needed moment to wonder—what is the "unforced rhythm of grace..." and where do I sign up to learn it?

Secondary Preaching Theme

Romans 7:15-25a

This passage reads like a Dr. Seuss book. "I don't know what I'm doing, because I don't do what I want to do. Instead, I do the thing that I hate...."

The bottom line is this: it is hard work to be human. We are fundamentally wired to *want* to do good, but somewhere between the wanting and the doing, the wheels come off. And there is that three-letter word that polite mainline protestants don't talk about—*sin*. Paul approaches this touchy subject from a global perspective. In spite of the singular language he employs, this is really his commentary on the broader human condition.

These verses are a continuation of the themes of Matthew 11: that faith offers more freedom than restrictions; and that the freedom found in the way of Jesus is a freedom *for* something; not just a freedom from strict moral code.

Real transformation, Paul reminds the Romans, is rooted in practice and relationship—not in following any one set of commandments. This would be a good opportunity to preach about mindfulness, intention, and the spiritual disciplines that help us move toward the "good" we so wish to do without being pulled away by the many things that distract and tempt us away from the work of transformation.

July 16, 2017

Genesis 25:19-34; Psalm 65:(1-8), 9-13; Romans 8:1-11; Matthew 13:1-9, 18-23

Preaching Theme

So this farmer went out with a bunch of seeds. And he scattered them far and wide. Some fell on the road, so the road runners ate them. Some fell on the red rock; those seeds sprouted quickly, but their roots didn't go very deep. They withered and died in the blazing sun, and the remains were trampled by coyotes. Some fell in the dry and thorny weeds; those seeds never had a chance. And some of those seeds fell on rich, fertile soil and grew forth abundant harvest.

That farmer must have lived in Arizona.

Many of us learned some version of this story when we were very small. As one of my elders said, "It's so rich and visual, you can just see the flannel board." Even if you didn't grow up in a faith community, you've probably heard a secular translation. These images can be easily applied to academics, business, family life, investment—any of which a preacher could incorporate for a particular context.

But for now, go back in time for a minute. You're five years old, and your Sunday school teacher says, "Now, children, which kind of soil do you want to be?" The answer is clear ... *the good soil*. ("Jesus" might also be a correct answer, as Jesus is the appropriate answer to any question asked in a children's sermon). Yes, we want to be the good soil. Now go back and sit quietly with your parents and *listen*—be good soil—and God will grow something beautiful in your heart.

Hey, don't pull your sister's hair in church. And that quarter I just gave you is for the collection plate.

Anyway ... it's a true and important message, that we need spiritual practices to make us "fertile soil" for God's word and God's will in our lives. Prayer. Scripture. Kindness and generosity. These things will make us the kind of ground where good things happen.

But maybe now, as grownups, we need to think also about what kind of *farmers* we want to be.

The right answer, of course, is the Kentucky kind. You want to farm in Kentucky where the "corn tops ripe and the meadows in the bloom," and the tobacco leaves are bigger than your head, and the tomatoes are really tomatoes, and the strawberries are crayon-red, and a five-minute run to the garden is all the dinner prep you need. That's what kind of farmer you want to be.

But the facts of life are, most of us are farming in Arizona. Metaphorically speaking, of course.

In the desert, you have to scatter your seeds—the gospel potential life and growth—far and wide. Because in reality, much of what you have is going to land in a barren place. It might look green enough right now...but wait till July and see where the sun hits. See what other-terrestrial bugs and reptiles and rodents come crawling out at night to graze. See what a few months of no rain does to that promising corner of the garden.

But there...just over there, that spot so utterly desolate and dry? There, exactly, is where the wildflowers come up singing in April. Where the winter grass pops up in December after just one hard rain. Where the cactus has been storing water, all year long, for just such a time as this.

You don't know where your stuff is going to land. In ministry, in relationships, in business, in art. The landscape of our every day is broad and varied. If you want life to emerge from what you have in your hand, you've got to toss it far and wide and generously, and trust God for the growth.

That's what kind of farmers we want to be, if we are people of faith. We've got to sow generously, knowing that we are letting go of much more than what we hold in our hand. In good faith, we let go of our possessions, our agenda, and all expectations of "where the good soil is." We let go, and watch in awe, as God takes our small seeds of faith and transforms them...ten, twenty, one hundred times over.

Secondary Preaching Theme

Psalm 65

Summer is a great time to preach a psalm (or several). Especially one as rich in imagery as this. Chances are you may have a light crowd, with Little League season in full swing, the call of yard work, and families scattered to the farthest corners on vacation. Worship can be light and life-giving in its simplicity.

Work in the rich soil of this text, maybe dwelling on that notion of being "filled full by the goodness of your house" (Ps 65:4). What does it mean to be content with the simple goodness of church life, of nature, and the sanctuary of our own homes?

If space allows, sensory stations might be set up all over the worship area. While music plays (Classical? Meditative? Chill acoustic?) have people wander through different sections of the psalm—a "waves" station with trickling fountains, an anointing, and/or an invitation to pour a drink for your neighbor. A "garden" scene with rich potting soil to dig your hands in, prayer rocks to take home, or beautiful images of nature. Maybe even have a place for people to experience the fresh "fruits" of creation, in this season of abundance.

Worship Helps

For Call to Worship, or Benediction, read Wendell Berry's "The Peace of Wild Things."

July 23, 2017

Genesis 28:10-19a; Psalm 86:11-17; Romans 8:12-25; Matthew 13:24-30, 36-43

Call to Worship

L: Come with joy, come with thanksgiving,
P: This is holy ground.
L: Bring your sorrow, bring your pain,
P: This is holy ground.
L: Speak words of blessing, pour out your gifts
P: This is holy ground.
L: Go rejoicing, go in new life,
All: This is holy ground.

Children's Blessing

God of our good gifts: grow your seeds of hope in the lives of these young ones. Nurture the unruly spirit of joy that they so want to share with us. Bless their noise, their play, their listening ears, that they might know the whisper of your love. Call them into fullness of life, leading them in the way that you would have them go. And may this church family be faithful stewards of their faith, entrusted to our care and keeping. Amen.

Preaching Theme

I lived in Arizona for seven years and know this to be true: after the blessed benediction of rain in the desert, there will be weeds. Abundant weeds. Where the earth is so parched, the first drop of moisture brings forth all manner of latent vegetation—from beautiful wildflowers to potent, allergen-bearing stuff. After a few early March showers, the wilderness comes alive, impossibly, with green growing things.

Following these bursts of spring precipitation, you start to dread each trip to the mailbox. Because you know what's coming: that little white envelope with the cellophane window. It bears a short, concise note: you've been fined twenty-five dollars for the *totally natural* life that has taken root on your front lawn. In the urban desert, "nature" is subject to approval by the neighborhood association.

Remember that parable about the seed that falls on rock and how it can't take root and grow because of the hot sun? Desert weeds did not get this memo. They flourish up through the landscaped gravel, the concrete pavers, the fake Astroturf, even the sizzling, cracked red clay. Call them a nuisance, call them an eyesore, but they are also a miracle of nature.

Jesus says you can move a mountain with the faith of a mustard seed. This image makes for the perfect children's moment or hands-on Sunday school lesson. What better way to teach a child that even small people, in developing stages of faith, have the power of God at their fingertips?

Small faith matters. But another small truth of the mustard seed bears telling: *mustard is a weed.* Unwanted, unruly, unlovely—and not matching the neighbors' landscaping.

Maybe, instead of praying for God to eliminate the weeds from our hearts, we might invite that Holy Gardener to come in and plant some. Let God nurture something within us that doesn't match the neighbor's yard, and that cannot be contained within the fence of our frail form. Grow something "wild and unruly," as the Dixie Chicks say.[2] Let faith be like scrappy desert weeds, coming up through the rocks and the cracks and the lifeless void, throwing a splash of green across the crumbling wilderness.

The kingdom of God is like Kudzu, and we are not the boss of it. Maybe "have faith the size of a mustard seed" (Matt 17:20) does not just mean small faith. Maybe it's faith that flourishes in wilderness and finds a way to thrive in unlikely places. Have *that* kind of faith and you can move mountains. Something so wild and free— you'd better believe God is working in that.

Secondary Preaching Theme

Genesis 28:10-19a

Every now and then, we come upon a place of undeniable holiness: a span of natural beauty; a grandmother's kitchen, where we feel safe and loved; a lovely worship space where we feel connected to God and community. When we enter such a place, we know we've come home.

Holy ground is not something we can build or buy—it is gifted to us. And yet, we spend much of our free time trying to *create* sacred space. Isn't that what we're doing when we spend hours cruising the aisles of Home Depot? Or scouring Pinterest and wondering how people have so much time on their hands? Even going to workshops or conferences or reading books about "how to make your worship space *super extra holy.*" At the heart of all this effort, we are dreaming of the perfect living room/yard/work area/sanctuary. Something holy.

But as Wendell Berry reminds us, "There are no un-sacred spaces; there are only sacred spaces and desecrated spaces."[3]

This is what people need to hear and be reminded of on those weeks when the newsfeed, or even our own communities, are full of unbearable pain and brokenness. There are no un-sacred places.

And the God of our being is not "up there," invisible at the top of some cosmic ladder. God is on the ground. And so are we, the church. Like Jacob, we've been gifted with holy ground—sacred community and the shared narrative of our faith—*so that* we might be a blessing to those who are hurting, lost, or alone. All this holiness—it can be neither created nor destroyed.

July 30, 2017

Genesis 29:15-28; Psalm 119:129-136; Romans 8:26-39; Matthew 13:31-33, 44-52

Gathering Prayer

Dear God, your kingdom has come near to us and yet in this world it can be difficult to see that same kingdom. We believe in your kingdom among us, yet it often seems hidden behind the sufferings that come, the tragedies that strike, the events that seem to proclaim that the powers of this world are all that matter. Give us eyes to see you and your kingdom and hearts to worship you at all times in the conviction that finally nothing will separate us from your love in Christ. Amen.

Preaching Theme

In Matthew 13 Jesus goes on something of a parable binge as he piles on one simile for the kingdom after the next: seeds, yeast, treasure, pearl, and a fishing net. Mostly all of this points to the apparent littleness of the kingdom—the kingdom can hide in plain sight. Tiny seeds disappear into the soil, yeast becomes indistinguishable from the larger lump of dough, the whole thing can be stumbled upon below the soil in some random field. The kingdom is real and will, in the longest possible run, be the ultimate reality for us all. But in the meanwhile, you could almost miss it. In fact, if we bring Matthew 13 alongside the epistle reading from Romans 8, we see how Paul needs to reassure his readers in Rome that nothing can separate them from God's love and he needs to do that precisely because there are so many big things in this world that surely look as though they could do the job of removing us from God's grip.

History is loud and noisy with persecutions and troubles and hardships and famines and wars. The newspaper does not generally proclaim the kingdom of God but instead trumpets all that is happening and going wrong with the kingdoms of people. And a lot of what goes wrong with earthly kingdoms surely can feel threatening to us Christians and definitely looks larger and more powerful than most of what goes on at your average church where the kingdom is preached. But nothing can finally touch the reality of God's kingdom and our citizenship in it. Jesus told these parables not just in order to describe the kingdom for us but also to reassure us: even when it seems weak or hidden, the kingdom is the greatest reality of them all and it is our joy if by grace we have the eyes to see it.

Secondary Preaching Themes

The Bible is a book of profound realism. Sometimes you see that when you bring certain passages together that you might otherwise tend to leave hermetically sealed from one another. But in this set of Lectionary readings we receive both eloquent reflections on the wonder and majesty of God's statutes/precepts from Psalm 119 and a story from Genesis that focuses on some people who seem to delight in trickery and living by their wits rather than following any lofty laws from God. Jacob has fled to Uncle Laban's ranch on account of his past chicanery in deceiving just about everyone he's ever known. But as he settles into his new life, he discovers in his mother's brother someone whose penchant for dirty tricks rivals his own! And it's going to go on like this for a couple decades, too, as both Jacob and Laban scheme night and day to get the best of the other. It's hardly a vignette of delighting in God's ways as Psalm 119 celebrates it! Yet the history of God's people is, therefore, a good example of why we needed not only God's law to guide our steps but finally also a Savior whose upside-down kingdom of service and humility (that we enter only by grace alone) would be the only way sinful, scheming folks like Jacob, Laban, and the rest of us would finally be able to live in ways that bring true delight to God and to us.

Prayer of Confession

Lord God, we profess to love your law and delight in your ways and yet we confess that our daily actions are too often a contradiction to that profession. We ask you to direct our footsteps but then veer off on side roads that seem more convenient to us at the time. We ask you to not let sin rule over us, yet we keep some of our dearest temptations close to hand some days. You shine your face upon us and by your Spirit display to us the flourishing that comes from following your ways, but sometimes we avert our eyes and do our own thing anyway. Forgive us, we pray. Have mercy upon us and restore us to yourself through Christ Jesus our Lord, who alone is our hope and whose ways we will once more try to follow every day. In Christ's name we pray. Amen.

Benediction

Go in peace to love and serve the Lord, knowing that nothing in all creation can separate you from the love of God that is in Christ Jesus our Lord. Hallelujah and Amen!

Outside the Door to the Christian Life

Matthew 13:44-46

O. Wesley Allen Jr.

It could be hard to be a Christian in the first century. Remember, back then most Christians were Jews: if you were a Jew who was a Christian, other Jews who didn't believe in Jesus said you sold out the faith and the traditions of Israel because you claim Jesus is the Messiah and allow Gentiles in your community. Or if you were a Gentile who was a Christian and other Romans saw you hanging around with Jews and talking about a Messiah, they said you joined a cult. They expected you at any minute to be hanging out at the airport with a tambourine, selling carnations, asking people if they're saved, and handing out pamphlets that explain five steps to get to heaven.

There was risk and cost to being a Christian back in the first century. You could lose family, friends, livelihood. In some rare circumstances, you might even lose your life.

Maybe you had joined the church thinking God would suddenly make everything go your way. Or maybe you thought Jesus would return on the clouds at any moment so it was okay if things were tough for a short period because you would be in paradise just over the next hill. But things weren't okay, and Jesus didn't return.

So the early followers of Jesus asked: Is it really worth it? All the sacrifices? All the danger? All the risks? All the changes? You've sold the entirety of your old life to buy into this new life. But is this new life worth it?

Well, Jesus still hasn't come back some two thousand years later, even though we check the weather report each evening to see if the local meteorologist says, "A warm front will move in to the Bluegrass overnight bringing with it overcast skies and the Son of God."

And it doesn't look like Christians today are any better off than the rest of the population. We struggle with finances and cancer and dysfunctional home life and depression and tensions at work and fear and prejudice just like everyone else. The rain falls on the just and the unjust alike.

But the problem isn't only that we are just like everyone else. No, we Christians are overachievers: we add some burdens that are particular to our faith on top of the burdens that come with just being human.

Small burdens like getting up on Sunday morning in the middle of the summer to come to church to hear a guest preacher when it'd be awfully nice to sleep in and wait until Bill gets back. Small burdens like reading scripture when we'd rather be reading a trashy novel. Small burdens like saying grace before meals in a restaurant when it's a little embarrassing.

But we Christians add larger burdens to life too. Like being honest on taxes when we could save hundreds of dollars. Larger burdens like giving more to charity than others do. Larger burdens of loving our neighbors as ourselves.

And of course there are some humongous burdens too. Huge burdens of loving our enemies, not just our neighbors. Huge burdens of daily taking up our crosses and following Jesus. Huge burdens of being peacemakers in a world of violence and hatred. Huge burdens of putting our highest loyalty not to family, tribe, or nation, but to the reign of God. Huge burdens of trying to answer the call, as Matthew says, to be perfect as God in heaven is perfect. John Wesley loved that line, so we strive daily, constantly, to do the will of God. And it's costly. It's risky. It's a burden.

I was teaching an adult Sunday school class discussion once where one person asked, "If someone were able to prove that there were no heaven or hell, would you still be a Christian?" Everyone—every single person—answered no. I was shocked and asked why they wouldn't be a Christian if they didn't believe in life after death. And they said life is a test. And God wouldn't be fair if God didn't reward some people for trying to do good and condemn others for bringing harm into the world. They knew how burdensome it is to live the Christian life faithfully.

> "The kingdom of heaven is like a treasure that somebody hid in a field, which someone else found and covered up. Full of joy, the finder sold everything and bought that field. Again, the kingdom of heaven is like a merchant in search of fine pearls. When he found one very precious pearl, he went and sold all that he owned and bought it." (Matt 13:44-46)

Jesus has been telling parables by the lakeside to the crowds. But after speaking in public, he tells some parables in private only to his disciples. They wouldn't make sense to everyone. They aren't for public consumption. They're specifically for the church, specifically for those burdened by the life of discipleship. The experience of discovering God's reign pictured in these two parables only makes sense to those already inside the faith, those who have given up so much to be in God's dominion, those who know the risks and burdens of the Christian life. Those who fear losing friends, family, livelihood, and even life for the faith.

But you know parables by their very nature have something odd in them. These twists are tricks on the hearer. You think you're trying to unravel the puzzle of the parable and suddenly you realize it's about you; you have become the puzzle; and you are being unraveled. Parables are riddles…about us.

Why would a man find a treasure in a field and then sell everything to buy that field when he could have just taken the treasure? That's not real smart. Why would a merchant sell everything he has to buy a single pearl? It's a terrible business plan to sell your whole inventory to buy one item!

Why would a person give up the ease of life in order to take on all the risks and burdens of the Christian faith? It's a terrible life plan. There are smarter ways to spend our time, our money, our energy, our loyalties; smarter ways to commit our prayers, presence, gifts, and service.

Well, you know jokes can go on forever, twisting and turning this way and that, but it's the punchline that makes the joke. The focus of any good joke is at the end, not the beginning. The same is true of parables. The selling of everything is the set-up, not the focus. The punchline is the field with a treasure hidden in it, which I now own. The punchline is a priceless pearl in my pocket. These parables remind the disciples, remind the early church, that they haven't really made sacrifices at all. In moving from their former life to the Christian life, they haven't given something up; they've traded up.

Loving our neighbors as ourselves. Loving our enemies. Taking up our crosses. Giving to the poor. Caring for the widow and orphan. Changing the world. These aren't the burdens of the Christian life. They are the rewards of the Christian life!

To be able to pray for those who persecute us instead of being filled with hate is a treasure hidden in a field. To be able to give our second coat to one in need or to walk the second mile instead of only being able to put ourselves first is a pearl of immense value. The Christian life isn't a test for which we're rewarded. The Christian life is the reward! Living out the Christian faith isn't a sacrifice we make to get into the reign of God; these are our experiences of being in the reign of God already.

Parables that unravel us and help us see ourselves in a new light aren't only ancient. There's a parable similar to those we read today that you may know. It doesn't come from Jesus. Oddly enough it comes from Franz Kafka,[4] who wrote the short story "Metamorphosis" you probably read back in middle school. But don't worry— this Kafka parable isn't about a man becoming a cockroach. It goes like this:

Before the Law [before the Torah], there's a doorkeeper on guard. A man from the country comes to this doorkeeper and prays to be let in to the Law. But the doorkeeper says that he can't let him in right now. The man thinks it over and then asks if he'll be allowed in later. "It's possible," says the doorkeeper, "but not at the moment."

Since the gate stands open, and the doorkeeper stands to the side of it, the man can stoop down to look through the gateway into the interior. When the doorkeeper sees him doing this, he laughs and says: "If you're so drawn to it, just try to go in despite my resistance. But take note: I'm powerful. And I'm only the least of the doorkeepers. From hall to hall there's one doorkeeper after another, each more powerful than the last."

The man from the country didn't expect all of this since he assumed the Law should be accessible at all times and to everyone.

He decides to wait, and the doorkeeper gives him a stool and lets him sit down at one side of the door. There he sits for days...and years. Over and over again he asks to be let in. He even offers bribes, but always the doorkeeper says no.

The man from the country grows old sitting outside the Law, and comes to a point where he realizes he doesn't have long to live. So he waves the doorkeeper over to him and asks, "Everyone strives to reach the Law; so how is it that for all these years no one else has ever come trying to get in?" The doorkeeper answers: "No one else could ever be admitted here, since this gate was made only for you. And now I'm going to close it."

Ugh. I know parables are meant to be riddles, but wow. It's unraveling to say the least. What are we to make of that story? What are we to do in light of that story? Maybe if we listen to it one more time, we can catch some details we missed before:

Before the Christian life, there's a doorkeeper on guard. You come from First United Methodist Church to this doorkeeper and ask to be let in. But the doorkeeper says that he won't let you in right now. You ponder this and then ask if he'll let you in later. "Maybe," he says, "but no promises and not right now."

Since the gate stands open and the doorkeeper stands to the side of it, you can stoop down to peek through the gateway into the Christian life. When the doorkeeper sees you doing this, he laughs and says: "If you are so drawn to it, just try to go in despite my resistance. But take note: I'm pretty strong. It will be a struggle to get past me. And I'm only the least of the doorkeepers. From hall to hall there is one doorkeeper after another, each more powerful than the last. It will be a burden to struggle with us all."

You stand there looking through the door and ask yourself, "Is it worth it? Is it worth the risk, worth the burden, worth the struggle to get in? I wonder if the struggle is a treasure? I wonder if the risk is a pearl?" And you take a deep breath, you shift your weight on your feet, and...

Amen.

August 6, 2017

Genesis 32:22-31 (Psalm 17:1-7, 15); Isaiah 55:1-5 (Psalm 145:8-9, 14-21); Romans 9:1-5; Matthew 14:13-21

Gathering Prayer

Dear God—Father, Son, and Holy Spirit—we come before you today from a world that is hungry to know you, to find you, to wrestle with you until some kind of blessing may come. We come hungry ourselves, yearning to feast on the bread that alone satisfies. Bread of heaven, feed us now in this hour of worship and always that we may be full of the knowledge of your grace and mercy toward us. In Christ we pray. Amen.

Preaching Theme

Sooner or later God meets us where we live. For crafty, scheming, heel-grasping Jacob, that meant God's getting down into the mud and blood of this earth and quite literally wrestling with the man who had devoted his life to getting ahead by being stronger and smarter than his every opponent. Jacob wrestled with Esau in the womb, wrestled with Esau out of the womb. Next Jacob wrestled with his father, Isaac, and then for about two decades had an ongoing wrestling match with his uncle–cum–father-in-law, Laban. God had stayed with Jacob through all that and even had made some pretty big promises to him at a place dubbed Bethel. But what Jacob did not yet know is what a lot of us are often slow to realize: the best things in life come by grace alone. The old self—the scheming, live-by-your-wits, pull-yourself-up-by-the-bootstrap self—has to die and only then can God bring us the blessing of a new identity. Jacob became Israel. In Christ we become children of God. Who knows what our particular Jabbok River will be—we all have a different "Jabbok," a different place of "Peniel" where we see God's own face and discover the glorious truth that grace alone ushers us into God's wonderful light. But God is as relentless as God is gracious and if we now live as children of the light, we can know for sure that our life is a sheer gift.

Secondary Preaching Themes

We live in a world of death, and this was a fact that crashed in on Jesus with peculiar force after hearing of John the Baptist's brutal beheading. John's death was so senseless, the result of a boozy, lusty, thoughtless offer by a corrupt king. So Jesus withdraws to another place of death—a lonely wilderness spot—only to be followed by masses of people hungry for Jesus's words and soon enough just plain hungry physically. But where Jesus goes, life follows (as Isaiah predicted). So when the people had eaten and were satisfied, they perhaps sensed that life is grace—in the wilderness but always. If we manage to find life in a world of death, it's all grace.

Once a person discovers the truth that God alone gives life by grace alone (as Paul did the day he stopped being Saul), then that person begins having a lifelong love affair with the gospel that reveals that grace. Once you have eaten the heavenly manna only God can give—the bread you cannot buy with money as Isaiah said—you want to share it with the whole world. For Paul in Romans 9, that meant sharing it with his fellow Jews who had not yet come to recognize Jesus as the Christ. Paul was so desperate to see also them fed that he said he'd go to hell himself if that's what it took to get more people to take a seat at Jesus's banquet table. Curiously, that actually *is* what Jesus did to accomplish that very goal.

Responsive Reading (Based on Psalm 145)

The Lord is gracious and compassionate, slow to anger and rich in love.

All you have made will praise you, Lord; your saints extol you.

The Lord upholds all those who fall and lifts up those who are bowed down.

All you have made will praise you, Lord; your saints extol you.

You give food at the proper time, you open your hand and satisfy our desires.

All you have made will praise you, Lord; your saints extol you.

The Lord is righteous in all his ways and loving toward all he has made.

All you have made will praise you, Lord; your saints extol you.

The Lord is near to all who call on him; the Lord watches over all who love him.

All you have made will praise you, Lord; your saints extol you.

Our mouths will speak in praise of the Lord.

Let every creature praise God's holy name forever and ever. Amen!

Benediction

The Lord bless you and keep you. The Lord show you his very face so as to be gracious to you. The Lord open his right hand so that he may feed you with the richest of fare, satisfying you with good things both this day and even forevermore. Amen.

August 13, 2017

Genesis 37:1-4, 12-28; Psalm 85:8-13; Romans 10:5-15; Matthew 14:22-33

Gathering Prayer (drawn from Psalm 85)

Lord our God, your salvation is near to us and so in worship we now draw near to you. We thank you and praise you for your righteousness, for your love, for your faithfulness, for your goodness. You are our God and we are your people, engulfed by your glory, awed by your holiness. Bless us by your Spirit as we now bring to you the harvest of praise that is your due as we worship you in the splendor of your glorious righteousness. Amen.

Preaching Theme

It is not difficult to see that crying out to the Lord is a common theme here. Had the Lectionary included the first seven verses of Psalm 85, we would be able to see more easily that the praises of verses 8-13 are premised on a cry for forgiveness and deliverance in verses 1-7. And then there's Peter letting his doubts quite literally sink him in Matthew 14 even as hapless Joseph cries from the cistern where his nasty brothers had dumped him in the Genesis reading. Overtop of all that are Paul's soaring words in Romans 10 about calling on the name of the Lord leading to salvation. But in truth it's not just this collection of passages that show our human need to call on God and be delivered: this is a Bible-wide motif.

It reminds me of something I heard the writer Anne Lamott say in a speech one time at Calvin College: "I basically have just the two prayers: 'Help me, help me, help me!' and 'Thank you, thank you, thank you!'" Sounds like the prayer life of most of us! Whether because of the perils of living in a still-nasty world where even brothers can turn on each other or due to the consequences of our own too-oft foolish (and sinful) choices, we routinely encounter the fear, the doubt, the pain, the disorientation that causes us to cry out "Help us, O God!"

Not long ago while I was visiting the 9/11 Museum and Memorial in New York City, I noticed something curious in the very first display visitors encounter. As you enter the museum, you see three or four pillars onto which a series of images from that terrible day in September 2001 are projected. Most of the pictures are of people, hands over mouths, looking up toward the horrors going on in the Twin Towers. From overhead there is also an audio loop of people saying where they had been that day, what they saw, how they felt. Strikingly, a large number of those eyewitness testimonies ended the same way: "I started to pray...I just prayed...I prayed." Life in this world means we are going to have lots of occasions to call upon the name of the Lord. The gospel's good news is that when we do so in faith, the Lord our God hears us and assures us again and again of our salvation. Thanks be to God!

Secondary Preaching Theme

Barbara Brown Taylor once preached a sermon in which she mused about Peter's grandstanding in front of his peers by stepping out of the boat to walk on water with Jesus. Of course, having that kind of courage—using Peter as a role model, in other words—is what a lot of people take away from the story in Matthew 14. As one popular book title put it, "*If You Want to Walk on Water, You Have to Get Out of the Boat.*" Be a risk taker! Step out on faith! Be bold for Jesus! But maybe there is something noble about staying in the boat and pulling on the oars too. Peter would not have been less faithful had he just waited for Jesus to join them in the boat (and he would have been spared a rebuke too). Once Jesus did climb over the gunwale and take a seat—calming the storm in an instant as he did so—all the disciples worshipped him as the Son of God he had so clearly revealed himself to be that evening (first in the feeding of five thousand people and now in mastering even the wind and the waves). Whether we try to do daring things in Jesus's power as Peter did or stay in the boat and do more ordinary tasks, recognizing Jesus as the Son of God and then giving him our worship is what it is all about in the church. We are perhaps not all called to try to walk on water, but there are lots of ways to be vessels of God's grace short of such big things. The main thing is to keep our eyes on Jesus no matter what we happen to be doing at any given moment.

Prayer of Application

We thank you, O God, for hearing us when we call out to you. But remind us, too, that for others to know you are available to receive also their cries, we need to proclaim you to them, to preach your gospel in deed and through our words. How can they call on you if they do not know you? Make of our lives, O God, a living testimony to your goodness. In Christ we pray. Amen.

August 20, 2017

Genesis 45:1-15; Isaiah 56:1, 6-8; Romans 11:1-2a, 29-32; Matthew 15:(10-20), 21-28

Gathering Prayer

O God, as we assemble today, we recognize that you are the one gathering us from east and west, north and south. We gather today not only to receive from you but to minister to you, to love your name, and to serve you. We come to you, the God of justice, righteousness, and love for the outcast. We ask that you would bring us joy today in your house. And, we thank you that your house is known as a house of prayer for all peoples. Amen.

Preaching Theme

In Isaiah 56 we are confronted with the mention of immigrants and outcasts. We all know what it is like to be on the outside looking in. We all know what it feels like to be left out of an inside joke or conversation. We all know what it is like to feel as though we don't belong somewhere. God's heart has always been for the outsider. Even when God was choosing to bless Israel, it was not at the expense of all the other nations of the earth. We tend to think in an either/or mentality as if God has to choose one nation over another. Instead, God chose to bless the nation of Israel in order that all the families of the earth would be blessed through them (Gen 12:2-3).

Notice the words of blessing for immigrants in this Isaiah 56 passage. They are active words, actions God will perform. God will *bring* them to his holy mountain. He will not merely hope that they come on their own. His welcome is intentional and proactive. God will *bring them joy* in his house of prayer. His desire is not that they simply tolerate or find a place to exist in his house, but that they rejoice and thrive. He will *accept* their sacrifices and worship. This is in direct contradiction to what was happening when Jesus saw the money-changers in the temple many years after Isaiah wrote these words. Jesus saw foreigners being excluded and taken advantage of and not allowed in the temple. And, he was angry about it and took serious action.

Secondary Preaching Themes

In all of these scripture passages we see a both-and acceptance and blessing. In Matthew, Jesus recognizes he was sent specifically to the "lost sheep of Israel" and yet, he honors the faith of a Canaanite woman and heals her daughter. In Romans 11, we see that even though God has wholeheartedly accepted Gentiles into his family, he has not rejected his own people, the Jews. And, he desires to have mercy on all. And in the story of Joseph in Genesis 45, we see that God blesses Egypt through Joseph (an Israelite). And, that God blesses the Israelites through Egypt.

Also in the Isaiah, Romans, and Genesis passages, we see God's control of the details of life. When we are left out with no place to belong, we see God as bringer and gatherer (Isa 56). We see God as the one who "locked up all people in disobedience, in order to have mercy on all of them" (Rom 11:32). When we have been mistreated by others, in Genesis 45, we see God as the one who sent Joseph ahead to Egypt (even though it was his brothers who sold him into slavery). Even in the difficult circumstances of life, we can rest in the fact that God is in control.

Illustration: Both Isaiah 56 and Genesis 45 reference someone who is outside of their country/culture of origin. Joseph was an Israelite living in Egypt. The people God is gathering into his house in Isaiah are "immigrants." To help illustrate this idea, it would be helpful to hear the story of an immigrant in your congregation or community.

Prayer of Repentance

O God, we recognize that you have gathered and welcomed us freely into your house. Forgive us for the times we have not welcomed others freely into your house. Forgive us for the times we have forgotten that we ourselves were once foreigners. Forgive us, for we have not intentionally brought outsiders into your house as you do. Forgive us, for we have excluded others with our words, our body language, our in-house rules, and our inaction. We agree with you that your house is to be a house of prayer for all nations.

Benediction

As you go from here, may you remember how you have been gathered and welcomed into God's house. No matter where you go, you have a place of belonging in God's house. May you know that you are blessed by God to be a blessing to others. May you look for ways to extend that blessing to the immigrants and outsiders around you.

August 27, 2017

Exodus 1:8–2:10; Isaiah 51:1-6; Romans 12:1-8; Matthew 16:13-20

Gathering Prayer

Most merciful God, we come before you today recognizing that in your mercy you have given us another day. Your mercies were brand new this morning when we woke up. We recognize that in your mercy, you have spared us the punishment of our sins and have paid the cost for our redemption. Your mercies are ours in Jesus. We recognize that in your mercy you have called us your people. Once we had not received mercy, but now we have received mercy. We have your mercy in our sights. As we would fix our eyes on a long-awaited loved one that we spot from a distance in a crowded airport, so we fix our eyes on your mercy. And, with your mercy in our view, we come today to offer ourselves to you. Amen.

Preaching Theme

As human beings, our natural tendency is to think of ourselves as right and everyone else as, well, wrong. The way we do things seems to us like the best way to do things. And it should. If you grew up driving on the left side of the road, then it will *feel* wrong to drive on the right side of the road. Your way is not necessarily better, but it will *feel* better to you. And, that is okay. What you do with that feeling is what matters. In Romans 12:3 we are challenged not to think about ourselves more highly than we ought. Notice that it does not say we are not to think about ourselves. Rather, it says, we are to think of ourselves reasonably. We are to think about ourselves in light of God's goodness and his work in our lives. We are not to pretend we don't have anything to offer. We are not to act as if we ourselves are the saviors of the world. We are to see ourselves rightly.

The scripture continues to say that we are many parts of the same body. God designed the body well and each part has a unique function. Don't compare yourself to someone else wishing you had what they have. Don't see yourself as less important because you aren't able to do the same things as those around you. You were created uniquely. Your gifts are unique. It is possible to spend so much time looking at what you don't have that you never take time to realize and appreciate what you do have. The truth is that we need you to do what you have been graced by God to do. And you need the other parts of the body to do what God created them to do. We need each other. "Individually we belong to each other," verse 5 says. Whatever gift you may have, you would do well to recognize it, understand how it fits with the other parts of the body, and offer it wholeheartedly for God's glory!

Secondary Preaching Themes

There is no gift, no profession that God can't use for his glory and to benefit his people. In Exodus 1:8-21 we see some unlikely heroes. In this passage, some God-fearing midwives carry out their profession in faith and faithfulness. As lowly service-oriented people, they stand up to the powerful. And, God blesses them. And, he uses them to bless and prosper an entire people. They did not say, "We are lowly midwives. What can we do?" They lived out their calling in faith and faithfulness. How might you leverage your gifts, your profession, your calling for the glory of God and the good of his people?

Also, we see clearly highlighted in Isaiah 51:2 that it is God's blessing that prospers us. We do not make ourselves. God is the one who prospered Abraham and made him the father of many nations. It is the same God who blessed the midwives in Exodus 1 and blessed the entire nation of Israel through them. It is the very same God who gives Peter revelation to understand who Jesus was and to speak the truth out so boldly and clearly in Matthew 16:17. And, it is the same God who graces us with different gifts as Romans 12:5 points out.

Dramatic Reading

READER 1: Your gifts do not depend on our efforts. Your grace does not rely on our will. When we were altogether unlovely, you loved us still.

READER 2: Your gifts do not depend on our efforts. Your grace does not rely on our will. When we were altogether unlovely, you loved us still.

TOGETHER: You have made us objects of your mercy, O God.

READER 3: Your gifts do not depend on our efforts. Your grace does not rely on our will. When we were altogether unlovely, you loved us still.

READER 4: Your gifts do not depend on our efforts. Your grace does not rely on our will. When we were altogether unlovely, you loved us still.

TOGETHER: You have shown the riches of your glory to us.

READER 1: We, who were not a people...

READER: 2: You called us *your* people.

READER 3: We who were not beloved...

READER 4: You called us beloved.

TOGETHER: You call us beloved.

September 3, 2017

Exodus 3:1-15; Jeremiah 15:15-21; Romans 12:9-21; Matthew 16:21-28

Responsive Reading

LEADER: This earth is groaning and in turmoil.

PEOPLE: Do you see, God? Do you care?

LEADER: Hatred runs rampant and ravages villages and homes and entire people groups.

PEOPLE: Do you see, God? Do you care?

LEADER: People created in your image are being treated as commodities, as inconveniences, as if they have no souls.

PEOPLE: Do you see, God? Do you care?

LEADER: The brokenness of our world is unavoidable.

PEOPLE: Do you see, God? Do you care?

LEADER: We are hard pressed on every side.

PEOPLE: Do you see, God? Do you care?

Preaching Theme

Our God is the God who sees. Our God is the God who knows. Our God is the God who rescues and delivers in his time and in his way. Though God works in the mundane and the ordinary, his ways are in no way ordinary. In Exodus 3, we see Moses in the midst of the mundane. He had simply shown up for work like he had hundreds, probably thousands of times before. He was caring for his father-in-law's sheep when all of the sudden something out of the ordinary caught his eye. He saw a bush that was in flames but not being burned up. Some of us, if we are honest, probably wouldn't have noticed that at all, because we are too consumed with our own agendas and lists of things to do. Others of us might have taken a picture of the sight and posted something on Instagram or Facebook, and then moved on with our day. Thankfully, Moses stopped what he was doing and decided to get a closer look. It seems (according to verse 4) that if he hadn't stopped to look closer, God might not have spoken to him that day. Instead, because of his curiosity, and his willingness to have his day interrupted, Moses heard God speak powerfully.

After telling Moses that he sees and cares and will deliver, God invites Moses into the process. It will be God's deliverance, in God's way. God will not only rescue the Israelites out of the land of Egypt but also bring them into a good land, a place of abundance. In verse 11, we see Moses's tendency (like our own) to make it about himself once again. God quickly counters by reminding Moses that it is not about the one being sent (Moses) but about the one doing the sending (God). Moses's job is to go to the Israelite elders and tell them about God's care for them and his plan to rescue them. Then, he is to go with the elders and be a spokesperson for God to the king of Egypt. Verse 20 makes it clear that it will be God's strength that saves the day.

Secondary Preaching Theme

God's ways are not our ways. And, sometimes, they go directly against our natural instincts. In Matthew 16, when Jesus says that in order to fulfill God's plan, he must suffer and be killed, Peter vehemently opposes the idea. It seems to Peter that there is no way that Jesus's suffering and death could be right or good. But Jesus indicates that this kind of thinking, though it may be natural, is in direct opposition to God's ways. He rebukes Peter strongly and says that he is not thinking God's thoughts, but human thoughts. According to God's ways, if a person wants to save his or her life, he or she must lose it for God's sake.

Romans 12 makes a long list of the ways God wants us to relate to others. Some of them are completely opposite to what we would think is right. "Welcome strangers into your home" (Rom 12:13). Really? Isn't that dangerous? After all, you don't know them or the kind of person they are. That seems unsafe, unwise. "Bless people who harass you," says verse 14. Our natural inclination is to defend ourselves and speak ill of those who hurt us. Maybe on a good day, we could see the benefit of holding our tongues and not saying anything at all since we have nothing nice to say. But God says we are to go out of our way to bless those who harass us. He goes on to say that if our enemy is in need, we should give him something to eat and drink. Clearly, God's ways are not our ways.

Prayer of Dedication

O God, your ways are higher than our ways. Your thoughts are higher than our thoughts. Give us eyes to see when our ways are in opposition to your ways. Give us faith and courage to exchange our plans for yours. You are mighty to save. May we be your spokespeople. We turn to you. May our mouths, our actions, and our very lives utter what is worthwhile. In the name of Jesus we pray, trusting your ability to work these things into us. Amen.

September 10, 2017

Exodus 12:1-14; Ezekiel 33:7-11; Romans 13:8-14; Matthew 18:15-20

Call to Worship (Based on Hebrews 10:19-25)

LEADER: Brothers and sisters, we have confidence that we can enter the holy of holies by means of Jesus's blood

PEOPLE: Through a new and living way that he opened up for us through the curtain, which is his body.

LEADER: Therefore, let us draw near with a genuine heart with the certainty that our faith gives us, since our hearts are sprinkled clean from an evil conscience and our bodies are washed with pure water.

PEOPLE: Let us hold on to the confession of our hope without wavering, because the one who made the promises is reliable.

LEADER: Don't stop meeting together with other believers, which some people have gotten into the habit of doing. Instead, encourage each other, especially as you see the day drawing near.

PEOPLE: And let us consider each other carefully for the purpose of sparking love and good deeds.

Preaching Theme

God takes sin seriously. And God calls us to do the same. Because of God's love, God does not ignore sin or pretend it doesn't exist. In Matthew 18:15-20, we are challenged not to ignore our brother or sister's sin but to confront it lovingly and, first of all, in private. We are to love our brothers and sisters by not publicly shaming them or gossiping to others about their sins. Instead, we should correct them when we are alone with them. God loves us enough to tell us truthfully what is harmful to our own souls. Love does not delight in evil but rejoices with the truth.

Love is not silent. We see in Ezekiel 33:7-11 that God warns people to turn from their wicked ways. Not only does God do this but God commands Ezekiel as his spokesperson to warn them as well. In fact, God goes so far as to say that if Ezekiel does not warn people to turn from their wicked ways, God will hold Ezekiel personally responsible for their death. God takes sin seriously. And God commands Ezekiel to do the same. God does not take pleasure in the death of the wicked. Instead, God desires them to turn from their wicked ways and live (Ezek 33:11).

Taking sin seriously, according to Ezekiel 33 and Romans 13, means that we should turn from it completely, getting rid of "the actions that belong to the darkness." Sin, in many ways, is like cancer. A little cancer may not affect your quality of life very much. But it spreads! I don't know anyone who is okay with the idea of just living with a little cancer. Because we know what that little bit of cancer could lead to. May we be increasingly more aware of what a little bit of sin can lead to. And, may we deal with it appropriately.

Secondary Preaching Theme

A spotless Lamb. When God is ready to deliver his people from the oppression of Egypt, he institutes the celebration of Passover. Deeply significant and symbolic, this celebration centers around the slaughtering of a "flawless" lamb. The Israelites are to kill the lamb at a specific, set time. Then, they are to smear the blood of the lamb on the doorposts of their houses. This is no laughing matter. God takes it very seriously. Sin leads to death. He is prepared to strike down the oldest children and animals as punishment for sin. But God provides a way of escape. He says that whenever he sees blood on the doorpost of a house, he will "pass over" that family. The blood does not symbolize that those people within the house are perfect or sinless. Instead, the blood on the doorposts symbolizes the fact that the people inside that dwelling have trusted God's word and provision on their behalf.

In the same way, Jesus is the spotless Lamb of God. His death on our behalf provides us with freedom from receiving the punishment for our sins. His blood allows God to pass over us when he is meting out judgment. Jesus's blood does not signify that we are sinless. By no means! Instead, it symbolizes the fact that we have trusted God's word and provision on our behalf.

Dramatic Reading

READER #1: Another day, another transgression. Another reminder that sin is ever-present.

READER #2: Still, you are pure, God, so perfectly blameless. And all of your judgments are true and righteous.

READER #1: We are at your mercy.

READER #2: We are at your mercy.

TOGETHER: We are at your mercy, O God.

READER #1: Another dawn, a promising sunrise delivering mercies anew with rays of vibrant light.

READER #2: God, you are faithful, so perfectly faithful. Because of your faithfulness we are not consumed.

READER #1: We are at your mercy.

READER #2: We are at your mercy.

TOGETHER: We are at your mercy, O God.

READER #1: You do not treat us as our sins deserve.

READER #2: You are rich in love.

READER #1: You do not treat us as our sins deserve.

READER #2: You have shed your blood.

READER #1: We are at your mercy.

READER #2: We are at your mercy.

TOGETHER: We are at your mercy, O God.

September 17, 2017

Exodus 14:19-31; Psalm 103:(1-7), 8-13; Romans 14:1-12; Matthew 18:21-25

Gathering Prayer

Loving and gracious God, open our hearts and our minds to the work of your Spirit, that you might illuminate our darkness and lead us to new hope and possibility. We acknowledge the many ways that we have fallen short of your best ideals for us and we thank you for your forgiveness and your faithful love. Amen.

Preaching Theme

Peter asked a fairly straightforward question: "Lord, how many times should I forgive my brother or sister who sins against me?" (Matt 18:21). He knew that Hebrew law only required him to forgive someone three times, so his question about forgiving someone seven times could have been intended to impress Jesus. ("I know I'm only supposed to forgive a person three times. But what if I forgive them seven? Double the number I'm required, plus one for good measure? I bet that would make me a pretty good disciple, huh?")

And Jesus knew it. He knew that Peter wasn't really asking how many times he should forgive, but why he should forgive. Out of selfish motivation? Sense of duty or obligation? And that's why Jesus answered the question in a most odd way: "Not just seven times, but rather as many as seventy-seven times" (v. 22).

To interpret Jesus's answer as a strict numerical calculation would be to miss the point altogether. It wasn't about how many times to forgive, but why. Remember the basic background behind the book of Matthew. It was written in the first century, mostly to a community of Jewish and Judeo-Christian people in the ancient city of Antioch. This was a book written to people with a clear understanding of Jewish stories and Hebrew narratives.

Matthew's audience would have been very familiar with the number seven. Every seventh day Jews would be commanded to rest, observe Sabbath, and restore themselves to health. Every seventh year they would be called to give the land a rest and restore it to nourishment. Every seventh cycle of seven years, on the year of Jubilee, debts were forgiven, slaves were released, and humanity was restored in their ancestral relationships.

The number seven would always convey to them a call to restoration, healing, and reconciliation. And in the Hebrew mind, participating in the number seven would be cosmic in nature, with universal consequences. It would be joining together in partnership with a God who brought order out of chaos in the days of creation and is always working to bring restoration, rest, and healing out of a broken world.

Jesus's answer blew Peter away—not because it suggested an astronomical number of times to forgive but because it expanded Peter's thinking about the nature and purpose of forgiveness.

The act of forgiving someone else for their offense may feel like a private matter in a singular relationship between two fairly inconspicuous individuals. But in Jesus's view, it is a sacred act, with cosmic implications. Forgiveness is a full participation in the activity of God to restore all creation back to its original health, wholeness, and state of goodness. If you think that forgiveness is just a small activity of human exchange, think again. Whenever you forgive, you participate in God's greatest ongoing project—the restoration of the whole world back to the way it was originally intended.

Secondary Preaching Themes

Paul's letter to the Romans acknowledges the potentially harmful ways that people in the church can exploit their differences. Rather than cast judgment on each other, Paul calls us to do all that we do "for the Lord," thereby uniting our differences around a common commitment to Jesus Christ. In a sense, Romans 14:1-12 underscores the Matthew text by describing ways that we can reconcile the brokenness of human relationships.

The famous story of the crossing of the Red Sea in Exodus 14 is the Hebrew Bible's most powerful reminder that God works to liberate the oppressed and to set the captive free. A connection can be made with the gospel text by reminding people that to forgive is to set free a relationship that has been held captive by bitterness and resentment.

Prayer of Application

O God, who created order out of chaos and called us to Sabbath rest, empower us by your Spirit. May we participate in your ongoing work of restoring creation to order and reconciling all things to yourself. Help us to forgive, just as you have forgiven us. Amen.

Benediction

May the God who led the Israelites to freedom

And called the church to faithfulness

Lead you to a place of healing

In your mind, your body, your spirit

And in your relationships with others.

And may you become an agent of healing

In a conflicted world

Full of broken relationships.

May you be an agent for reconciliation

Through the love of God,

The power of the Holy Spirit,

And in the name of Jesus Christ,

Amen.

September 24, 2017

Exodus 16:2-15; Psalm 145:1-8; Philippians 1:21-30; Matthew 20:1-16

Gathering Prayer

Gracious and eternal God, we thank you for the privilege of being part of your church. You have created us with a diversity of gifts, perspectives, and potential, and you call us to be one in Christ. Empower us this day to live lives worthy of your gospel. Amen.

Preaching Theme

On school playground blacktops across the country, a familiar scene unfolds. A group of children are waiting to be chosen for a game of basketball. Two of the kids are captains, widely known for their playing skills, their athleticism, and their dominance of the sport. One by one, they alternate selecting members of their team, always beginning with the children who are the better ball handlers, more accurate shooters, and skillful rebounders. These are the children who are always among the first to be chosen.

Then, the pool of eligible kids inevitably shrinks to the last unfortunate few. These are the kids who trip over their feet when they dribble, who shoot the ball while launching a prayer, and who can't run down the court without stopping to catch their breath. They are the ones chosen last, the ones who the captains pick because they have to, not because they want to.

When the teams are chosen, there is always an automatic hierarchy. The ones picked early get the ball, the attention, and the acclaim. The ones chosen later are lucky even to be on the team and are hardly in a position to assert any privilege.

When Jesus told a story about some laborers in Matthew's Gospel, the same dynamics are at play. The ones chosen first have been working the longest, putting in the most time, and therefore expect to receive the highest regard from the master, let alone the most pay. The ones chosen last, later in the day, should feel fortunate they even found work to begin with. They haven't put in as much work, and therefore should not expect as much reward.

But like many of Jesus's parables, the zinger is not only surprising, it is unconventional and transformative. In the economics of the kingdom, God's love is not dispersed according to merit. It is equally shared, regardless of works, and regardless of worth. It is as if the schoolyard captain is saying to each player on the team, "It doesn't matter when you were selected, it doesn't matter how well you play, and I don't care how well you think you can do. You are on my team now, and that is all that matters."

Secondary Preaching Themes

The Exodus text is the story of the manna in the wilderness, in which God graciously grants provision to the grumbling, starving Israelites. The gift has one caveat: one can only gather enough food for a day's time. It will not keep until the next day, but there will be enough for everyone to get their fill one day at a time. This story can certainly reinforce the economics of the kingdom described in the gospel passage, as God's grace shows no favoritism or preferential treatment, and cannot be stockpiled by some at the expense of others. God loves all with equanimity and shows great compassion to the weak and less fortunate in a world where power differentials exist.

Paul challenges the church in Philippi to "live together in a manner worthy of Christ's gospel" (Phil 1:27). In a culture where people are fractured along polarized extremes, Paul encourages everyone to "struggle together" and remain "united in one spirit and mind" (v. 27). Rather than live like kids picking teams in a school yard, we are to live together as one people, under the loving hand of a God who generously granted us the privilege of suffering for Christ's sake.

Images: The movie *Sandlot* is a story about a band of boys playing baseball in their neighborhood sandlot every summer. It is told from the perspective of Scotty Smalls, a new kid without any demonstrable proficiency in the sport. Despite their initial hesitation, the other boys embrace him as one of their own, and he winds up being a greater benefit to the team than they first expected.

Prayer of Application

Merciful God, forgive us for the many ways that we have built barriers of division among us. Call us to a life united by your Spirit, and remind us that in your generosity, we are all equal recipients of your faithful love. Renew our commitment to serve each other and to love you in all that we do. Amen.

Benediction

And now may the one who chose you

Not by merit or worth,

Or by popularity or preferential treatment,

But simply by God's lavish grace alone

Call you to live in harmony with one another.

May the one who created you in God's image,

Saved you through God's Son,

And granted you strength through God's Spirit,

Guide and direct you through the living of these days,

Amen.

October 1, 2017

Exodus 17:1-7; Psalm 25:1-9; Philippians 2:1-13; Matthew 21:23-32

Gathering Prayer

Eternal God, we thank you for the gift of your holy scriptures, whose timeless truths always bring a relevant word to our ears. Prepare our hearts and minds with a ready willingness to hear its truths, heed its calling, and enact its lessons. Amen.

Preaching Theme

The scripture reading from Philippians is widely considered by biblical scholars to be one of the earliest Christian hymns. In some translations, the text is set apart in the form of song lyrics, to make it look like one is reading a poem or the lyrics to a song. We can assume that both Paul and early Christians were familiar with these words as Paul quoted it in this letter to Philippi.

It is a song that captures the full salvation story: How Jesus, the second person of the Godhead, equal with God the Father, came down to earth and became human. He did this not out of selfish gain, but out of humility, obedience, and service, for the sake of humanity. This is a passage about the servanthood of Jesus Christ and God's call upon all of us to give our lives in service to others.

It is interesting that in many computer word-processing programs, the word *servanthood* is not included in the standard, built-in vocabulary. That means that whenever one types the word on their computer, and when the spell-correct function is turned on, there is a red squiggly line underneath the word to indicate that you misspelled it. That red squiggly line is a visual reminder to us of just how foreign a word, and foreign an idea, *servanthood* is to the culture at large.

- We don't understand why someone would want to seek the benefit of others, and the community around them, rather than their own interests.

- We don't see why someone would want to use their skills and abilities for the sake of others, regardless of payment or compensation.

- We don't see why someone would choose not to be served, but to serve.

- We don't understand why some people would want to lose their life in order to gain it, or choose to be last, instead of first.

But that's what happens when the cross gets ahold of you. It takes your priorities and your life and turns them upside-down. We are called to be servants, regardless of how strange it might seem to the world around us. We are each given a unique set of skills, and a specific set of abilities, to serve others and offer ourselves for the benefit of those in need. Whether we know it or not, we can be servants, just like Jesus.

Secondary Preaching Themes

Both the Exodus text and the Gospel text have the common theme of "questioning authority." In the case of the Israelites, they were challenging Moses out of their thirst for water. "Why did you bring us out of Egypt to kill us, our children, and our livestock with thirst?" (Exod 17:3). They were physically desperate, but their confrontation was ultimately a theological one: Where was this God in the midst of their suffering?

Likewise, the Pharisees and religious officials came challenging Jesus on the basis that he was performing his ministry. Their antagonism was essentially an exploration of how they might trap him; instead, they wound up trapping themselves. Ultimately, Matthew tells us that the question of authority was a losing proposition for them. Both texts teach us that when times are at their most desperate, the temptation to test God must ultimately take a backseat to trusting God. Even though we cannot understand God's ways, we must learn to trust in God's presence, power, and authority over our lives.

Prayer of Application

Holy God, you created us in your image and breathed into us the breath of life. Enable us therefore to embody your example of self-sacrificial love, that we may seek to serve, rather than to be served. Help us to see your image in the lives of others around us, so that our every deed of service may be an act of worship of you. And may our efforts be deemed worthy of the grace that has saved us and the calling you have placed upon our lives. Amen.

Benediction

And now may the God who raised Jesus from the dead

Bring forth new hope out of your despair;

May the Jesus whose mind was set in humility and service

Call you into your unique path of servanthood;

And may the Spirit of God whose fruit draws believers together

Unite you with the mission of the church,

Which sends you out to build the kingdom

One step,

One moment, and

One life at a time.

Amen.

October 8, 2017

Exodus 20:1-4, 7-9, 12-20; Psalm 80:7-15; Philippians 3:4b-14; Matthew 21:33-46

Gathering Prayer

God of our ancestors, you called forth your people from slavery in Egypt and led them to new life in the promised land. Call us to obedience in this moment, that we might follow you through the wilderness into a future with hope. Amen.

Preaching Theme

The Ten Commandments is one of those iconic elements of our Judeo-Christian heritage that has crossed over into our secular and pop-culture consciousness as it has come to symbolize for many a certain kind of ethical and religious conviction. Those who believe that the Ten Commandments should be displayed in public areas contend that this country needs to return to a strict adherence to Judeo-Christian morals. On the other hand, there are those who believe that the Ten Commandments are less something to be displayed and more something to be lived out. One thing that both sides can agree on is this: in a culture today that has been slackened by radically individualized standards of conduct, the Ten Commandments offers a community ethic based on mutual commitment to God and a shared observance of human dignity.

Regardless of how polarizing the debate over the display of the Ten Commandments has become, it still remains one of the most important aspects of the Christian faith. Jesus's summary of the commandments in Mark 12:30 reduced the Ten Commandments down to two: love God and love others. In other words, we are not only to pursue wholeness and health in our "horizontal" relationships with other human beings, we are to be fully reconciled in our "vertical" relationship with God. It is impossible fully to have one without the other, for we can only love others when we fully love God, and vice versa.

With the addition of that love that Jesus's summary provides, the Ten Commandments become less a list of "dos and don'ts" (which is a common perception) and liberate a community to interact freely and joyfully with each other in the security of mutual respect, without fear of harm. In a sense, the Ten Commandments function like the fence of a playground, in which children can enjoy the freedoms of interacting with other children if they simply stay inside the clearly marked boundaries.

Secondary Preaching Themes

There was certainly no mistaking the interpretation that Jesus intended when he shared the parable in Matthew 21:33-46. In fact, the text offers one of the few times when the Gospel writer makes it explicitly clear what Jesus was saying: he was the son of the landowner, and the chief priests and Pharisees were the tenants. Jesus's words appear to be antagonizing, threatening the religious leaders with the imagery of a stone crushing them. But the parable is meant to be reverential, drawing attention to the power and glory of God: *"The Lord has done this, and it's amazing in our eyes"* (Mark 12:11). Too many Christians perceive the evangelical task to be one of debate and antagonism. Instead, our task is not to argue people into the kingdom, but to simply bear witness to the love and grace of God so that God's activity may be "amazing in their eyes."

Paul offers a compelling résumé of his history and heritage: circumcised on the eighth day, from the tribe of Benjamin, a "Hebrew of the Hebrews," a student of the Law, and blameless in its keeping. But all of those things paled in comparison to knowing Jesus Christ as his Lord and being made righteous in Christ through the power of the resurrection. And though one might perceive Paul's transformation as a singular moment in time, verses 12-14 portray the spiritual life as a constant journey of regular commitment and constant determination—a process rather than a precise moment.

Prayer of Application

Eternal and holy God, we thank you for the many ways you have brought order out of chaos. You call us to be a community brought together by the bonds of mutual respect and love; forgive us for the many ways and numerous instances when we have fallen short of your ideals. Forgive us for the times we have been envious, committed adultery, celebrated murder, failed to honor our ancestors, and violated your commandments in other ways. We wish to bring you the honor that you deserve, and we seek to love others in the ways you have loved us. Empower us by your Spirit to fulfill your will for our lives. And help us to become the community you have called us to be. Amen.

Benediction

And now may the God who called us out of the wilderness

Guide you through the living of your days.

And may you come to know the saving power of the resurrection

That you might live out your conviction that Jesus Christ is Lord.

And may the strength of the Holy Spirit

Empower you to bear witness to God's love in the world

That it might be amazing in the eyes of all whom we meet,

In the name of God the Father, Son, and Holy Spirit,

Amen.

October 15, 2017

Exodus 32:1-14; Psalm 23; Philippians 4:1-9; Matthew 22:1-14

Prayer for Illumination (Based on Psalm 23)

We pray, Lord, that as we listen to your word, we will hear our Shepherd's voice. May your rod and staff bring us both comfort and correction, and may your Spirit guide us on the proper paths so that we may live in gratitude to the invitations we hear from you today. Amen.

Preaching Theme

There's a lot of emotion flying around Mount Sinai. Down below, the Israelites are getting a little antsy to know what's next from their "new" God and their new leader, Moses. When they can't wait any longer, they return to the familiar: Aaron and statue gods. With the comfort of something to literally hold on to, shaped by their own hands and contributions, the people celebrate and throw a party, relieved to be comforted. Up the mountain, Yahweh's raw jealousy falls on lonely, vulnerable Moses. Standing between the righteous anger above and the raucous rejection below, Moses pleads on the only foundation he has: who God has revealed God to be. First, Moses tells Yahweh that God's reputation with the nations is at stake (does Yahweh want to prove the Egyptians right?), then Moses pulls out the big guns and puts God's words back on God: "You yourself promised, 'I'll make your descendants as many as the stars in the sky. And I've promised to give your descendants this whole land to possess for all time'" (Exod 32:13). It works! God remembers and keeps God's promise as God does not destroy the people who have let their emotions and worries disconnect them from their Savior God. When all seemed lost, Moses turned to the only thing that is sure: what God has promised. When it didn't seem as though God was keeping that promise, Moses wasn't afraid to remind God (through prayer) about those promises. God always keeps promises even if the people of God let themselves be led astray or worry themselves into a pit of despair—thank God that there was someone in their midst who knew to build their future on God, not humanity.

Secondary Preaching Themes

Like the Israelites at the bottom of Mount Sinai and the initial wedding guests who don't respond to the second invitation to the party, we seem to find it easy to forget that the king of kings is the one saving and inviting us to a new way of life. Who turns down an invitation to dinner from royalty? The ungrateful and disrespectful, that's who. Who forgets the God who brought down ten plagues and led you through the sea on dry ground? The ungrateful and the worrying, that's who. Yet that's basically what we do today when we go about our everyday tasks without a thought for God.

In Philippians 4, Paul describes both the response we usually give and the response God wishes to receive. First, there is the anxious one who has forgotten to pray because of his or her worries. Though their enemy lay at the bottom of the sea, the Israelites were in totally new territory once they left Egypt; the worry of the unknown led them to create their own comfort. Those who ignored the invitation to the wedding party were more worried about their businesses and crops than they were about offending the king; still others went further in their ungratefulness by killing the king's messenger. Second, Paul provides the prescription that would have done both the Israelites and the guests invited by the king some good: "Focus your thoughts on these things: all that is true, all that is holy, all that is just, all that is pure, all that is lovely, and all that is worthy of praise" (Phil 4:8). If the Israelites would have done so, the party they threw could have been focused on the God of their salvation from slavery, not some golden substitute. And if those wedding guests could have seen the purity of the loving king who was offering to welcome them into his joy, they too could have experienced gladness.

Prayer of Repentance (Based on Philippians 4)

Jesus, our firm foundation,

Though you are always near, we confess that we let our worries turn us from you.

Though you are always listening for our prayers, we confess that we try to solve our problems on our own.

Though you await us with peace, we confess that we do not treat others the way you taught us to. We fail to live in your gladness.

We bring our confessions to you and seek your forgiveness so that we can stand firmly on your peace.

In Jesus's name we pray. Amen.

Dedication/Charge (Based on Philippians 4)

Stand firm in the Lord.

We will be glad in the Lord always!

Do not be anxious.

Instead we will pray.

Practice what you have been taught.

We will love one another and think on these things.

Receive the peace of Jesus Christ.

We will stand firm in the Lord.

October 22, 2017

Exodus 33:12-23; Psalm 96:1-9; 1 Thessalonians 1:1-10; Matthew 22:15-22

Call to Worship/Opening Before Hymn of Praise (Based on Psalm 96)

Sing to the Lord a new song!
Sing to the Lord all the earth!
Sing to the Lord! Bless his name!
Share the news of his work every single day!
Declare God's glory among the nations.
He is awesome.
Give to the Lord
glory and power.
Give to the Lord
the glory due his name.
We enter God's courts now with our songs of praise.

Preaching Theme

We are agents of influence for God. Paul tells the church in Thessalonica that their testimony of faith, resilience, and living in trust and hope in Jesus has spread all over the region. In fact, people are talking to Paul and his travel companions about the Thessalonians before Paul even has a chance to use them as an example in his teaching and encouraging of other followers of the way! Trace the cycle of influence: Paul was converted on the road to Damascus and then offered his life to the people of Asia Minor as a living testimony to the grace and power of God. The church in Thessalonica received in faith the testimony Paul presented and experienced the empowering of the Holy Spirit, becoming imitators of Paul. Now, Paul has left them and is checking in by letter, overwhelmed with gratitude for how far the Spirit has taken them in sanctification. As a result, they have become an example from whom the message of God rings out loud and clear to Macedonia and Achaia and beyond. Paul tells them that they have truly given themselves over to God as they wait for Jesus, the Son, to return. He also lays out where all that power comes from: the power of the

Holy Spirit. It is the gift of faith that leads them to work in honor of the Lord; the gift of love that motivates their efforts; the gift of hope that sustains them to persevere in spite of their suffering. The followers of the way in Thessalonica have done a lovely job of giving to God what belongs to God; by doing so, they are living testimonies, able to encourage and influence others to see that trusting in the knowledge of God's choosing and love is the way to live in the Spirit's power.

Secondary Preaching Themes

The church in Thessalonica increases the influence of Jesus in the world, but the Sadducees in Matthew 22 were seeking to end Jesus's influence in Jerusalem. Knowing the unsteady political climate of the empire, the Sadducees were hoping to trap Jesus into either inciting the government or inciting his would-be followers. But, like so many who try to discredit Jesus and his influence in the world, they fail. What's interesting is that in their attempt to trick Jesus, they express the truth about him: Jesus doesn't care what other people think of him and he "[teaches] God's way as it really is" (v. 16). The Sadducees think that they can control him, instead of realizing what the people in Thessalonica realized: accepting and submitting wholeheartedly to God works much better.

Moses is also dealing with an influence problem. His problem, though, is that he is doubting his role as God's chosen agent of influence within the Israelites. Moses instinctively turns again to Yahweh for a sign that will fuel his faith, asking for a commitment of God's loving presence to fuel his efforts and relying on that hope to help him persevere through the challenges of leading God's people. Our amazingly compassionate and patient God sustains Moses's request, because, unlike the Sadducees who are trying to trap or manipulate Jesus, Moses is in a true relationship with Yahweh and is asking for the strength to carry out God's will. Just as the gifts of God sustain the church in Thessalonica and enable them to proclaim the glory of God, God gifts Moses with what he needs to carry out what God asks of him. As it was with them, so shall it be with us.

Image: Lee Strobel's testimony of coming to faith in Jesus ties together the themes of influence found in these passages. Lee's wife became a Christian, and the transformation of her character, which Lee described as winsome and attractive, was his first step into a church—albeit with the intentions of getting his wife free of the influence of the community of faith. But that Sunday he heard the message of the gospel and through the power of the Holy Spirit, experienced the deep conviction Paul describes as influencing and shaping the Thessalonians for God's glory. What had begun as an attempt to discredit the Christian faith led to Strobel's writing *The Case for Christ*, a proclamation of Strobel's personal faith and transformation. It has influenced many others to become believers around the world.

Offering Prayer

O Lord, we know that we are entrusted by you with all that we have and possess. We humbly offer to you these small gifts and ask for your blessing as we seek to faithfully give back to you what has always belonged to you. May our gifts be used for your kingdom. Amen.

October 29, 2017

Deuteronomy 34:1-12; Psalm 1; 1 Thessalonians 2:1-8; Matthew 22:34-46

Preaching Theme

Haddon Robinson has become well-known in preaching pedagogy for his concept of the big idea, meaning that each sermon should be about one main thing, fed and developed by all of the other points you make. What is so effective about a big idea is that has to be both broad and sharp—able to be applied by members of a diverse community. This week's set of lectionary texts all connect around this one big idea: obedience to God is paramount.

The Psalms begin with this wisdom: instead of falling to the peer pressure of the wicked, the happy person follows God's instructions, living in the knowledge that the Lord is intimately acquainted with their choices. Moses doesn't get to enter into the promised land because of his failure to obediently trust God's provision (he enacted God's miracle in such a way that maximized his role and downplayed God's; see Num 20), but he still receives grace from Yahweh, who allows him to see the promised land before dying. Paul tells the church in Thessalonica that his ministry is all about following God and that they only have to look at how he and his ministry partners have conducted themselves to see that their obedience is to God, not to the wicked that Psalm 1 describes.

In the Gospel text, Jesus pairs the summary of obedience to God's commandments with a question about their ultimate source, challenging those who hear him to encounter the one who fulfills the Law and the gospel in their midst. So yes, obedience is paramount. We obey because Jesus, who is greater than merely being the Son of David, commands it as the way to keep God at the center of our existence. We obey because there are consequences to our sins, as Moses experienced. We obey because wisdom means knowing that loving God's instructions is what leads to happiness and growth. We obey because, whether we realize it or not, we are missionaries with our lifestyle as well as our message.

Secondary Preaching Themes

Paul's reflection on his ministry in Thessalonica can be seen as the living embodiment of Psalm 1. Consider these echoes: Paul says God knows their hearts. They persisted even when they were insulted and they are not worried about anyone else but God and God's message being glorified.

As a further nuance to the big idea, Moses's story also shows us the abundant grace of God. One might be tempted to read Moses's and Yahweh's encounter on Mount Nebo with bitterness. How could God let Moses get so close and then take it away? Why would God taunt him so? The fact that Moses is silent throughout the whole story doesn't solidify a particular interpretation. But in remembering who God is, we can see Moses's experience on Mount Nebo as one filled with grace: God gave him the gift of seeing where the promise would be fulfilled, despite all of the people's—and his own—disobedience.

Image: Though not a perfect parallel to Moses and Yahweh on Mount Nebo, I had a pair of friends in college who chose to legally marry earlier than they planned because her mother was on her deathbed. The family gathered for a small ceremony in the hospital, gifting the dying mother with a picture of peace for those who would live on after her passing. Not technically needed or deserved, it was a gift borne out of deep love. Having led the people of Israel out of the struggle of slavery, through the turmoil of the desert, what a gift that picture of the peace of the promised land must have been to Moses.

Responsive Reading (Based on Matthew 22:34-46)

What is the greatest commandment in the Law?

To love the Lord our God with all our heart, with all our being, and with all our mind.

What is the second great commandment?

To love our neighbors as ourselves.

Who teaches us how to live these commands perfectly?

Jesus, our Lord. More than just the Son of David, he is the Messiah.

Prayer of Repentance (Based on Matthew 22:34-40)

Merciful God, we confess that we find it difficult to love and serve you fully. We have held on to parts of our hearts for ourselves, reserving some of our passion to pursue our sinful desires. We have turned down or ignored opportunities to serve those in need and have withheld our whole beings from being agents of your kingdom here on earth. We have let our minds wander away from wholesome and pure thoughts and have even acted on some of those sinful ideas. In all these and more, we have failed to love you with all that we are and have. Because we have not loved you fully, we have failed to love our neighbors as you commanded. Knowing that you are the God of love, we come to you now, seeking not only your forgiveness but also an infilling of your Spirit to enable us to love and serve you. In Jesus's name we pray. Amen.

Benediction

May God be your witness, may God be your courage, as you share your life with the world in honor of Father, Son, and Holy Spirit. The Lord is intimately acquainted with you and will guide you, now and forever. Amen.

November 5, 2017

Joshua 3:7-17; Psalm 43; 1 Thessalonians 2:9-13; Matthew 23:1-12

Lament Prayer (Based on Psalm 43)

Lord God, in frustration and discouragement we turn to you. We need to know that you are near, protecting and rescuing us from the false things others are saying. We are sad to live in such a world where people have the power to make us think you have rejected us. We know this is not your truth! We know you have made us to belong to you! We know that we are safe with you! Send your light and your truth to our minds when others make us falter and cause us to waiver. May we find refuge from the accusations and attacks in your presence. Fill our minds and our hearts with joy again. You are our Savior. May that hope sustain us through the trials of this world. Amen.

Prayer for Illumination

Lord God, open our hearts and minds, our eyes and our ears to receive these words as more than just a human message, but as the message of you, our God. By your Holy Spirit, enable the message we hear today to continue to work in our lives. In Jesus's name we pray. Amen.

Preaching Theme

When your leadership comes from God, stays focused on God, and is about pointing to God, things are likely to go immensely better. Notice what God tells Joshua: "Today I will begin to make you great in the opinion of all Israel" (Josh 3:7). Then Yahweh instructs Joshua to command the priests to carry the ark of the covenant across the flooded Jordan River. When it's time for Joshua's first foray into leadership, notice what he tells the people: "Listen to the words of the LORD your God" (v. 9). Instead of saying, "This is how you'll know that I have been chosen by God to lead you" (which is basically what God said to him), Joshua says, "This is how you will know that the living God is among you..." (v. 10). Joshua doesn't focus on establishing his own authority in this exercise of faith, and he doesn't command the priests to act out of his own authority. Instead, he keeps talking about Yahweh, about God's role as the ruler of the earth, about God, the one who is among them. We are all leaders in some capacity. Parents lead their homes, workers can lead by example in their workplace even if they are not the boss, teachers lead in their classrooms. The list could go on. Some of these environments are most suitable for outright expressions of faith; others require a subtler, lead-by-example approach. The principles we see Joshua exhibit remain the same: let God shape your role, stay focused on God's call for you in that particular place, and in all things, seek to give God glory.

Secondary Preaching Themes

Similarly, Paul's letter to the Thessalonians opens with a long address about his leadership because he had to leave their community sooner than any anticipated and he had not been able to return. One could say that he was trying to gain some leadership capital back. What Paul really wants to do, though, is get them thinking less about him alone and more about the one who sent him. Thus, Paul's authority and leadership in Thessalonica is justified through the witness it provides to God: Paul and his partners in ministry preach "*God's* good news," not Paul's good news. While they were in town, they acted as a father does, nurturing and instructing in the fear of the Lord with all of their pleading, encouraging, and appealing aimed at helping the people in Thessalonica to live God's call for them. Finally, Paul's happiness was not the result of having convinced more people to his message but that the people accepted what was taught as more than just his message: they understood it as God's message.

The Matthew text serves as the warning about what happens when leadership loses its focus on the things of God. Leaders can have the right knowledge and the wrong practice, thereby throwing their authority out the window. Jesus says that the Pharisees of his time had become less about exalting and pointing to God and more about making sure people knew how great they were. They went beyond what God required for them and for the people, exaggerated their religious expressions, and sought to be honored more than they encouraged God to be honored. They would have done well to practice what they preached. In verse 8, Jesus speaks directly to all who see themselves as his disciples: keep the one with ultimate authority at the top. Point always to the one teacher, Father, and Christ by submitting to serve your community as God calls you to do. If we submit ourselves to serving God and neighbor, the Holy Spirit will empower us for the roles of leadership God calls us to, and we won't have to assert our authority. Instead, others will experience and acknowledge God's authority and presence in us.

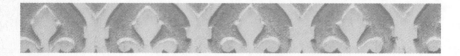

November 12, 2017

Joshua 24:1-3a, 14-25; Psalm 70; 1 Thessalonians 4:13-18; Matthew 25:1-13

Gathering Prayer

Gracious and giving God, your children are gathered together to thank you for who you are! As we pour out ourselves, we ask that you fill us, your lamps, with the oil of your Holy Spirit. Clear away the cluttered spaces in our hearts to make room for you. Increase our understanding of what you are speaking to us through your holy word. As we live to become more like our Savior, Jesus Christ, let our time together with you further prepare us for the Great Wedding Feast upon his return. In his wonderful name we pray. Amen.

Preaching Theme

For many of us it is easy to believe that when we have "plenty of time," we can delay doing the work we need to do leading up to the task or goal. Whether writing a paper for school, setting up for a special event that we may have helped to plan, or getting dressed to keep an appointment, it is very easy to think "I can prepare later." When we waste time or fail to anticipate that something could derail our plans, our "plenty of time" can disappear into "it's too late." The five foolish bridesmaids in Matthew 25 discovered this when the oil in their lamps had burned out by the time the bridegroom's arrival was announced.

Although they did not know when he would appear, they may have thought they had plenty of time, yet they neglected to consider that they may not have had enough fuel to shine their light through the night. The five wise bridesmaids had as much and as little information as the five foolish bridesmaids. But they were prepared. And they were wise enough not to allow their unwise counterparts to prevent them from enjoying the wedding feast with their groom.

As Jesus warns us in his parable of the ten bridesmaids, we do not know when he will return to claim his bride, his faithful followers. While we go about the busyness of life, we must understand that we must be intentional to "fill our lamps" every day. We always need more of his word; more of the Holy Spirit; more fellowship with our heavenly God. While we are dressing for the Great Wedding, we want Jesus to know who we are when he comes.

Secondary Preaching Themes

The text from Joshua reminds us that all humankind has a choice: we may follow those "gods" that distract us from becoming who God creates and calls us to be or we may choose to live for, follow, and serve God. This choice is not an intellectual choice, nor is it a "one and done" decision. When we remember what God has done for us, what God is doing for us every day in real time, and what God promised to do for us in the future, we should declare that we will live our lives for God, committing to make Jesus Christ the Lord of our lives. Once we make the Lord the center of our lifestyle, we will be prepared for his return.

When the follower of Jesus Christ diligently seeks God in life, receiving his saving help through our Savior, we have reason to freely rejoice as the psalmist declares in Psalm 70. We may also be encouraged as Paul shares in his letter to the Thessalonians that even in death, we may be spared grief, knowing that believers, living and deceased, will be caught up to live in heaven eternally.

Prayer of Application

Wonderful Father of heaven and earth, we thank you for your mercy and patience with us. We ask you to bless us with your wisdom. Keep us from deceiving ourselves into believing that we have plenty of time to prepare for your Son's return. Let our increasing love for you and your ways motivate us intentionally to seek more of you in the way we live and treat your people. Write your instructions on our hearts and teach us by your Holy Spirit to live into your teachings. Fill our lamps so that the flames that shine your light through us are bright, bring warmth to a cold world, and never burn out. In the name of our true Lord and Savior, Jesus Christ, we pray. Amen.

Benediction

May the preparation for our eternal home be joyous as we go out into our own worlds. May we draw on the presence of God without reservation or concern for what others think of our walk with God and without compromise by the trivial things we sometimes believe are important. May God the Father, God the Son, and God the Holy Spirit guide us, fill us, give us more. Amen.

November 19, 2017

Judges 4:1-7; Psalm 90; 1 Thessalonians 5:1-11; Matthew 25:14-30

Gathering Prayer

Loving Father, you deserve all of our praise, love, and attention. You are welcome in this space and in our lives. Speak plainly to us, Lord. Help us to understand what you want us to know as we are gathered together in your wonderful presence. As we leave our baggage with you, strengthen us by your Holy Spirit so that we will leave our worrisome burdens with you and not try to take them back. Keep us free to hear you and to allow you to mold us into your image. In the mighty name of Jesus Christ we pray. Amen.

Preaching Theme

The one-talent man in Jesus's parable of the Matthew passage is a fairly common character in real life. In this story he is a person who was given an asset based on his capacity to multiply it. His fellow servants, who apparently had greater gifts for investing, clearly understood what was expected of them when their boss gave them money before his journey. The one-talent man, however, may or may not have understood his delegated task. Because of his fear, because he was distracted by his lack of faith, and because of his perception of the boss's dishonest business dealings, he buried his asset in the ground.

This wicked servant may not have expected the boss to return at all. He was certainly unwilling to risk losing what he had been given. In the end, he lost far more than a single coin. He lost his future. He was cast into darkness.

True followers of Jesus Christ are called to be obedient to God. We are to be fruitful, growing in faith and trust in God. This is what God expects of us. Fear should never keep us from our mission to serve the Lord. When we trust in God when God commands us to live out God's instructions, we have no reason to be afraid of the outcome because God determines the outcome.

When we choose not to trust God, to judge God based on our limited understanding of his character and ways, we can also expect to be eternally separated from God instead of reigning in heaven with Christ.

Secondary Preaching Themes

The Apostle Paul declares that Christ's followers are not children of darkness but of light. In the presence of God's light, there is no space for fear. When we strive to live in God's light, we can see the signs of Christ's return. We can pursue Christlikeness with the assurance that we are protected by the armor of God. The helmet—our hope of salvation—protects our minds from foolish thoughts that give space to those events or experiences that distract us so that God can lead us in wise preparation for continuous fellowship with our Lord.

Psalm 90 and the Judges passage help us better understand how precious the time God gives us really is. We do not have time to waste on being afraid to carry out the commands God gives or to do the work he charges us to do. King Barak was afraid to go to battle without Judge Deborah. Not only did his fear motivate him to delay his obedience to God but he also wasted time. Every day, we should echo the psalmist's request for the Lord to teach us to be wise with our swiftly fleeting time so that we please him as a practice.

Responsive Reading (Based on Psalm 90)

People: Lord, you have been our help, generation after generation.

Leader: Before the mountains were born, before you birthed the earth and inhabited the world—from forever in the past to forever in the future, you are God.

People: You return people to dust because in your perspective a thousand years are like yesterday past. You sweep humans away like a dream, like grass that is renewed in the morning.

Leader: Yes, we are wasting away because of your wrath and are paralyzed with fear on account of your rage.

People: All our days slip away because of your fury.

Leader: Our years go by so quickly and then we fly off.

All: Teach us to number our days so we can have a wise heart!

People: Fill us full every morning with your faithful love so we can rejoice and celebrate our whole life long.

Leader: Let your acts be seen by your servants; let your glory be seen by their children.

People: Let the kindness of the Lord our God be over us.

All: Make the work of our hands last!

Prayer for the Offering

Generous Lord, we praise you for every asset with which you bless us. Knowing that all that we have—including ourselves—belongs to you, increase our faith and trust in you as we pay our tithes. Help us give our offerings joyously, without being afraid of whether we will have enough to live on in the coming week. Multiply what we return to you, O God, so that your kingdom on earth will be rigorously advanced. Thank you again for your love and provision! In Christ's name, we pray. Amen.

November 26, 2017
Christ the King Sunday

Ezekiel 34:11-16, 20-24; Psalm 95:1-7a; Ephesians 1:15-23; Matthew 25:31-46

Gathering Prayer

True Lord Jesus, we declare that you are Lord of all! We celebrate your sovereignty in all the earth! Our hearts are joined together in praise for your indescribable love for us! Help us, Lord, see you in humility and power! In your name we pray. Amen.

Preaching Theme

The Apostle Paul prayed many wonderful prayers for the early church. His heart was molded around the new Christians becoming increasingly devoted to growing in their new way of life in the risen Savior. Light is a very important image in his desires for his emerging congregations. In his prayer for the congregation at Ephesus, Paul shared that he was praying that the eyes of their hearts had light. How important it is for God's people to be able to see not only with natural eyes but with enlightened, discerning eyes. We can only see the un-seeable when we are walking in God's light, with our eyes wide open.

Through Christ, we gain the power of God. Our own purpose is revealed through him. Our ability to walk in our purpose comes through the empowerment of the Holy Spirit. We cannot "see" who we are truly called to be as members of the body of Christ without the Lord opening our eyes. How often do we miss the activities of God in the middle of all the bad news stories of our world because we are unable or unwilling to see the invisible miracles he performs every minute? How can we understand that as the body of Christ, we have victory over the ailments, crises, and trials that Jesus overcame on our behalf?

Believers need to see everything that God wants to show us. Like Paul, we should pray that the eyes of our hearts are full of light and open to see who we are in Christ Jesus.

Secondary Preaching Themes

Christ our Shepherd is gentle and loving, yet he will judge the nations for the condition of our hearts and according to how we love the ones he places in our paths. In Matthew and Ezekiel, Jesus is described as the shepherd who will separate the goats from the sheep.

The shepherd protects the sheep of his pasture. They are those who are bullied and bucked at by the bigger, stronger sheep. Yet they have the ability to see what others may not notice. Their gentleness resembles that of the one who cares for them. Their meekness and willingness to care for the marginalized resembles that of their companion. Such will enjoy the kingdom of heaven. The psalmist who wrote Psalm 95 makes the declaration that all of us who worship God are the sheep of his divine pasture.

When the king in Matthew 25 passes judgment on the sheep and the goats, each group offers a question that begins with "When did we see...?" In ministry, in our families, among our loved ones, and in life, we encounter and sometimes become "one of the least of these." Such folks do not always appear that way, however. We often do not "see" because some of us have created little painted boxes that define for us who the "least of these" really are. The persons described by Jesus are certainly included among those whom we may consider to be those uniquely in need of ministry. But what about the well-dressed career person who is secretly fighting deep depression with unauthorized prescription medication? Or the strong person with the beautiful smile who is hiding the cuts on their wrist under shirt cuffs after surviving a suicide attempt? Are we missing some of the least of these because they don't fit our image? Or are we diligently listening, loving, and intentionally looking for the Christ who needs ministry through us?

Responsive Reading (Based on Psalm 95)

Leader: Come, let's sing out to the Lord! Let's raise a joyful shout to the rock of our salvation!

People: Let's come before him with thanks! Let's shout songs of joy to him!

Leader: The Lord is a great God, the great king over all gods. The earth's depths are in his hands; the mountain heights belong to him.

People: Come, let's worship and bow down! Let's kneel before the Lord, our maker!

Leader: He is our God!

All: And we are the people of his pasture, the sheep in his hands! Amen.

Prayer of Application

Wonderful, knowing God, we thank you for giving us the light of Christ today. We pray like our brother Paul before us that you would push out the dark places and fill our hearts with your wonderful light. Open the eyes of our hearts so that we may see clearly those who need a listening ear, a visit, a plate of food, safe shelter, a prayer for healing, an encouraging word. Open our eyes to those whom we may introduce to your Son who supplies all these needs. Keep us from incorrect perceptions and placing unrealistic images in our little definition boxes. Thank you again, Lord, for hearing and answering our prayers. In your name we pray. Amen.

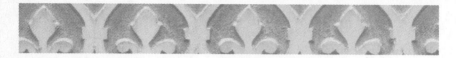

December 3, 2017
First Sunday of Advent

Isaiah 64:1-9; Psalm 80; 1 Corinthians 1:3-9; Mark 13:24-37

Gathering Prayer

Father God, thank you for your blessing in this Advent season. While we once again wait for the Messiah with the saints of old, remind us of the gift we have in your Son today, while we watch, serve, and wait for our risen Savior's return. Continue to stir the joy in our hearts while we anticipate our newest beginning. In the name of the one true Christ we pray. Amen.

Preaching Theme

We share in Isaiah's excitement in chapter 64 as he rehearses in his poetry the greatness of God. The prophet of old celebrates God's awesomeness, whose very presence can change the makeup of heaven and earth. Even when the Lord was angry over the sins of Israel, his wrath was not the final word. There was yet hope; there would yet be a new beginning. Because in his great love for us, he forgave our sins and embraced a broken, dysfunctional, and peculiar people.

When we have messed up so much that we don't know if there is any peace left in the world, because of Jesus Christ, there is a pause. There is a change in our condition that we may not immediately experience but that is as sure as God's promises. The past evaporates. The present drives into a hope-filled future. In Isaiah 64, we find that interruption in a verse that tells us, "But now, LORD, you are our father" (v. 8).

"After we have sinned against you, Lord; after we have rejected you to your face; because the shed blood of Jesus cleaned us up, now, Lord, you are our Father." *Now,* Lord. We are reconciled and restored to God because of the Savior who is here and for whom we are waiting.

Secondary Preaching Themes

Asaph knows that our restoration comes in the salvation we have in God. As he shares his lament over the oppression of his enemies and complains about the hard-knock life led by his fellow Israelites, he knows that God has the power to restore what sin has torn down.

Relationships?

Restored.

Happiness?

Restored.

Every need?

Restored.

Forgiven.

Purified. All by the power of a mighty, yet merciful God who defends his fallen, fickle people.

Mark and Corinthians remind us that we may be found blameless—innocent of wrongdoing—when we persevere in our calling to be obedient to God through Christ Jesus. As we live into the word of God, not only will our changing character testify for us but the power-filled Christianity we live will shout our testimony on earth and in the heavens. When the shout from the heavens is heard throughout all creation, we will be ready to be caught up in the air on our way to our celestial home.

Benediction

God, when we return to the communities from which you drew us today, bless us in our waiting. Open our eyes so that we will see Jesus wherever you send us, even in our homes. Remind us that your compassion and your salvation plan through our Lord Jesus restore our relationship with you. Don't let us ever take that divine gift for granted. Renew us, restore us while we anticipate the coming King. In Jesus's name we pray. Amen.

December 10, 2017
Second Sunday of Advent

Isaiah 40:1-11; Psalm 85; 2 Peter 3:8-15a; Mark 1:1-8

Gathering Prayer

King of kings, you who are the Valley Lifter and the Mountain Flattener, we bow the knee to your coming. We say, "You are God and there is no other—the one who is, and who was, and who is to come." Become the weightiest reality in our lives. Through our worship and our repentance, may a road be made for you. In Jesus's name we pray. Amen.

Prayer of Illumination

Thank you, Lord, that these are not empty words, flimsy or light. Thank you that these words are weighty and real, enduring forever. Holy Spirit, do your work through your word. Amen.

Preaching Theme

When the king comes, everything changes. Before paved roads, when a dignitary traveled, laborers were sent out to make the commute decent. For governors, rocks are removed and potholes patched. But for a pharaoh or an emperor, a highway is built—wide and straight. Teams of engineers ensure the monarch's procession does not go around the boulder; instead, the boulder must go. The monarch dips not into a gully; the gully must meet the road.

The preparations for Isaiah 40's King, however, dwarf imagination. Huge mountains are coming down. Grand canyons are being raised. This is not just any king—this is The King. *And his glory will be revealed.*

Glory! The whole chapter swoons before it (cf. God's size [vv. 12, 22], wisdom [v. 14], power [vv. 15, 23], intergalactic shepherding [v. 26]). We don't have human analogy for this kind of glory. Verse 10 says that he comes "with a triumphant arm."

But what's in those strong arms? A scepter? A sword? No, "he will gather lambs in his arms / and lift them onto his lap" (v. 11). That's true glory.

Glory has to do with weight. Isaiah's question is, "Will this coming King be the weightiest reality in your life or not?" The weeks before Christmas display what our culture glories in. Black Friday shows it—we're impressed by stuff and deals. Our Christmas newsletters show it—we are impressed by good looks and travel, successful kids and matching sweaters. But Isaiah says, "Do you not know? These things are dandelion puffs; their glory nothing."

Will the coming King be our weightiest reality? N. T. Wright put the question starkly: "That the hurricane has become human, that fire has become flesh, that life itself came and walked in our midst—Christianity either means that or it means nothing. It is either the most devastating disclosure of the deepest reality in the world, or it's a sham, a nonsense, a bit of deceitful playacting. Most of us, unable to cope with saying either of these things, condemn ourselves to live in the shallow world in between."[1]

The "shallow world in between" says it's fine to hear these lectionary texts in an Advent service, but we mustn't take it too far. None of that talk that this King is going to make a serious difference on how I shop over the holidays. None of that talk that this King determines how I think about myself (rather than the scale, the degree, the kids). None of that exclusive talk that he's the One Truth all peoples and cultures must bow to.

How real, how weighty, is the King's coming to us?

Secondary Preaching Themes

In Mark 1, John the Baptist saw clearly the implications of the King's coming. Sins must topple. Hearts must bow, and then rise up, dripping with the waters of repentance and a commitment to live differently.

Image: Every year I watch a Santa movie with my kids, and every year I squirm. There's something disconcerting about a message of "Just believe. Don't grow up and bah-humbug Santa. To keep the wonder of Christmas, just believe." What's a poor kid to believe? What's the content of that belief? That a weight-challenged fellow indulges folks with what they don't need to boost the economy every December 25? Fa-la-la.

I'm sorry but there's not much there to drive the engines of belief on. Not much that could ever bring "peace on earth, goodwill to men." *Polar Express* or *Miracle on 34th Street* demand wonder and belief, but there's no real weight behind it.

What if you could have all the wonder that these movies are proposing—and it actually gets better as you grow older because it just gets deeper, and wider, and higher, and broader, and closer—because the news is actually *true*?

What if there was a storyline worth "going up on a high mountain, and lifting up your voice with a shout," a storyline that has changed the lives of billions of people because it's actually *true*?

What if we can have more than the shallow, plastic world of Santa and instead see the dazzlingly brilliant God of God, Light of Light, true God of true God, who for us and for our salvation came down from heaven to be our King?

Now *that* will drive belief. That's the engine for wonder and change.

Benediction

May the blessing of the King—eternal, immortal, invisible, the only wise God—come to you, comfort you, and keep you. To him be honor and glory forever and ever. Amen.

December 17, 2017
Third Sunday of Advent

Isaiah 61:1-4, 8-11; Psalm 126; 1 Thessalonians 5:16-24; John 1:6-8, 19-28

Gathering Litany

The anointed King comes to be good news:

to bind up broken hearts, to announce the year of the Lord's favor.

So let those who plant with tears

reap the harvest with joyful shouts.

Let those who cried on the way, sowing their seed,

come home with songs of joy, bringing in the crops.

Call to Confession

Sometimes we enter worship with buoyant hearts, ready to belt out the hymns and laugh in the narthex. But other times we enter this place and all the motions of worship are on auto-pilot because our hearts are numb.

When we sit in the ash heap, scripture gives voice to that exact place of hurt and darkness. Let us confess our need, our tears, our ashes before the Lord.

Preaching Theme

Isaiah 61 puts a sputtering, smoldering candle before our eyes. It's the Hebrew word *keheh. Keheh* means an almost extinguished light, a breath away from smoke and ash. *Keheh* is the word picture for despair (v. 3).

Every time we face another Charleston, Newtown, or Syria, *keheh* is right there. Bad news sits with us as we sit in the pew. And the news of Isaiah 61 feels like so much airy-fairy preacher-talk.

When Israel first heard this message, she was that smoldering wick. She was in captive exile: lost children, lost home, lost identity, lost confidence that the Lord still gave a rip. And in this hopeless situation, Isaiah trumpets, "Captive mourners, look up!" Broken hearts will be pieced together. Handcuffs clatter off. Someone gives balloons for those Kleenex. And on the balloons are written "Congratulations! It's the Year of Jubilee!"

What is this year, also called the "Year of the Lord's favor"? At Mount Sinai, God knew folks would get stamped down by life and whole generations would end up smoldering. So he commanded one year in fifty to be set apart as a year of erased debts, returned family property, rest for the land itself. The old ash heap transformed into a garden of joy.

In our text, it's the Spirit-drenched Anointed One who ushers in Jubilee and as such, the text leads us straight to Luke 4. In Luke 4, we see Jesus proclaiming "in the power of the Spirit" (v. 14).

In Jesus, we witness Isaiah 61's Jubilee. Like an Old West trading post, Jesus exchanges lepers' disease for health. He takes the fetters of Nicodemus's legalism and hands him freedom. He takes the hard eyes of a prostitute and gives tears. Jesus still exchanges: our emptiness for his adventure; our bondaged wills, our bandaged hearts, our smoldering spirits for Pentecost freedom and fire.

Why does Jesus do this? He does it so "they will be called Oaks of Righteousness, planted by the LORD to glorify himself" (Isa 61:3). Isaiah 61 is not pie-in-the-sky. This is our reality. This is our bread and butter. Jesus *is* turning the tables on the evils of this world. The bad-news headlines, the Charleston gunshots, the *keheh* of our lives does not have the last word.

Advent gives us the last word. And this we proclaim: the good-news word that God became man in order to take the bad news of this world into his own hands and have them nailed to the cross and die because of it.

Secondary Preaching Themes

The anointing of Isaiah 61 was not only for Christ to "be a herald and witness of God's grace," as Calvin wrote, "but also for his whole body.... This anointing was diffused from the Head to the members."[2] John, in Mark 1, shows what an anointed herald and witness looks like: one who doggedly points beyond herself to the good news of Jesus.

The texts of 1 Thessalonians 5 and Psalm 126 both call forth songs of joy. The epistle does so in the midst of struggle, with an eye to the faithful one's coming that puts all things right. The psalm sings its songs after the gospel reversals arrived. (Notice the *forte* echoes between Isaiah 61 and Psalm 126.)

Image: Some in our congregations may say, "Pastor, I don't have the makeup of an oak. I feel more like that smoldering wick. Look. All I've got are ashes."

Sometimes it's hard to tell the difference. Weigh a handful of ashes and a single acorn on the scale and there's only a few grams difference. The burden placed on your hand will feel equal.

But if anyone is in Christ, even the grief, the very suffering, we experience has more an acorn quality about it than a useless ash quality. The contrast couldn't be greater. The ash is total annihilation and nothing will come of it. But in the acorn, all the power of the oak is present.

Prayer

Oh floweret bright, you still come to us amid the cold of winter, still in the darkness of night, and you bring hope. You bring healing. By the cross, you make us acorns. Thank you for being exactly the kind of God you are. In the good news of Jesus's name we pray. Amen.

Benediction

For as the soil makes the sprout come up and a garden causes seeds to grow, so the sovereign Lord will make righteousness and praise spring up in you before all nations.

December 24, 2017
Fourth Sunday of Advent, Christmas Eve

2 Samuel 7:1-11, 16; Psalm 89:1-4, 19-26; Romans 16:25-27; Luke 1:26-38

Call to Worship (Based on Psalm 89:1-4 and 2 Samuel 7:16)

I will sing of the Lord's loyal love forever. I will proclaim your faithfulness with my own mouth from one generation to the next.

Your kingdom will be secured forever before me. Your throne will be established forever.

That's why I say, "Your loyal love is rightly built—forever! You establish your faithfulness in heaven."

Your kingdom will be secured forever before me. Your throne will be established forever.

You said, "I made a covenant with my chosen one; I promised my servant David: 'I will establish your offspring forever; I will build up your throne from one generation to the next.'"

Your kingdom will be secured forever before me. Your throne will be established forever.

Preaching Theme

For a teacher and a text so full of explanation, it is important to note that Paul's letter to the Romans ends on a mysterious note. In a season of gift-wrapped presents and happy secrets kept, Paul's framing of the gospel as mystery can receive its proper hearing. On this last day of the Advent season, we may enjoy the expectant tension because we know Christmas morning resolution is coming. We'll finally be able to tear the paper off our preparation in order to discover that, at last, "all the hopes and fears of all the years are met" somewhere and by someone, somehow.[3] Just as tiny hands will destroy the wrapping paper to be delighted by the gift beneath, so too our mysterious God is turned into a mystery revealed in Jesus Christ. Just as you might hope for sentimental tears or whoops of joy from a gift unwrapped, so Paul hopes for the doxology, the praise, of the people who receive Christ as their gift. "May the glory be to God, who alone is wise! May the glory be to him through Jesus Christ forever! Amen" (Rom 16:27).

Secondary Preaching Themes

Paul reminds us that God's ways are mysterious. Nowhere in scripture might we say that is more true than the mystery of God becoming human flesh and doing so by way of an ordinary Jewish girl. This is, in the flesh, the act of a God who is not content to stay distant, to stay removed, even to stay entirely mysterious. This is, in the flesh, the act of a God who wants to be revealed, made known, born among us. The mystery of nine months in a womb, of waiting and wondering what sort of child this might be—a waiting and wondering known to many parents but also, now, known to us as we near the time in the church year for Jesus to be born. We wonder at the mystery as, in hushed, reverential tones we sing, "What child is this?"

We must be careful, of course, not to preach as though the triune God was secreting himself away, hiding from the people of Israel, while they sought for their redeemer. In Psalm 89, the people sing about a God who is distant in power yet present in love. They speak of a God who is faithful, who makes and keeps covenants, who is known to them from generation to generation. While Jesus Christ is a decisive in-breaking of God to the world, utterly unique, it is not the first or the only time God has loved and cared and reached down from the heavens.

In 2 Samuel, God reminds David, through Nathan, that "I have been traveling around in a tent and in a dwelling" (7:6). God moves with the people, makes camp with the people, stays with the people always. God guides through pillars of cloud and of fire. God delights to be near, though even in God's nearness, there is mystery. That same Hebrew word for *dwelling* is applied to Christ's incarnation. The God who has always dwelt with the people now dwells among them.

Doxology

God of our Advent waiting, you prepare your people with the words of poetry, prophecy, and history.
May the glory be to God, who alone is wise! May the glory be to him through Jesus Christ forever!
God of our Advent longing, you are not content to stay far away. You are as near to us as newborn flesh and a baby's wailing.

May the glory be to God, who alone is wise! May the glory be to him through Jesus Christ forever!

God of our Advent mystery, no human word or understanding can contain you but you are shown to us, revealed among us. In humble anticipation, we dare to proclaim: **May the glory be to God, who alone is wise! May the glory be to him through Jesus Christ forever! Amen.**

December 25, 2017
Christmas Day
Isaiah 9:2-7; Psalm 96; Titus 2:11-14; Luke 2:1-14, (15-20)

Prayer of Confession (Based on Titus 2:11-12)

Gracious God, in Jesus Christ you offer us salvation, healing from sin, and the Spirit's power to live a new life. You long to teach us what is right. But often we are careless and, other times, we are willful in our pursuit of those things that do not honor your name or lead us to joyful life. Forgive us and teach us to live sensible, ethical, and godly lives right now. Amen.

Assurance of Pardon (Based on Titus 2:13-14)

On this Christmas morning, our waiting is over. Christ is born to us, revealing our blessed hope of salvation. Hear these words and know God's power to heal, save, and forgive: "He gave himself for us in order to rescue us from every kind of lawless behavior, and cleanse a special people for himself who are eager to do good actions" (v. 14).

Preaching Theme

Before Isaac Watts ever penned a verse of "Joy to the World," the people of God knew it completely in Psalm 96. "Let earth receive her king"[4] sounds like "Bow down to the LORD in his holy splendor! Tremble before him, all the earth!" (v. 9). It's all in there. "Let heaven and nature sing." Blessings bestowed far as the curse is found and, especially, that the nations will know the glories of his righteousness and love. Let heaven celebrate! Let the earth rejoice! Let the sea and everything in it roar! Let the countryside and everything in it celebrate! He is coming to establish justice on the earth! He will establish justice in the world rightly. He will establish justice among all people fairly. The beloved songs of the season teach us what is right and true about our God. They give to God the glory due God's name. On this first of the two greatest feast and celebration days in the Christian year, God is bringing joy to earth. God is filling the whole creation with song, if we know how to listen for the tune. God is establishing truth and righteousness through the person of Jesus Christ. As preachers, it is always our task on this day to "repeat the sounding joy."

Secondary Preaching Themes

Psalm 96 names both the heavens and the countryside as places for God's people to rejoice. Through this lens, we view the appearance of angel choirs to lowly shepherds in Luke 2. The heavens and the countryside united in praise. And the praise of heaven comes down to echo throughout the city of Bethlehem as much as the shepherds say, "Let us go…let us confirm." Then, "The shepherds returned home, glorifying and praising God for all they had heard and seen" (v. 20). The echo reverberates throughout the world.

The overtones of Psalm 96 are rich in military language, of justice and the nations. There is joy in knowing that authority has come to rest on the shoulders of a king at last. But not just a king, says Isaiah 9, but this God is also a Counselor, a Father, and a Prince. When Christmastide falls upon countries at war, as it seemingly always does, the joy of the Holy Day is to remember that another day is coming, another kingdom—visible in shadows—will dawn in brightest light. It takes imagination and practice to live toward this song of praise but, Isaiah 9 lets us know, the coda of all our songs is accomplished by the zeal of the Lord.

Congregational Prayer (Based on Isaiah 9:6-7)

Holy God, today we rejoice in the child born to us, your Son, Jesus Christ. You have promised that the authority of the world will be on his shoulders. Therefore,

Establish your kingdom, O God.

The zeal of the Lord will accomplish it.

Wonderful Counselor, we need your wisdom to fill our lives. Give us discernment as we follow you. Comfort us in sorrow. Soothe those who struggle with temptation, with mental illness, those who suffer abuse, who desire reconciliation in broken relationships.

Establish your kingdom, O God.

The zeal of the Lord will accomplish it.

Mighty God, we need your will to direct our church. Teach us to care for the lost, the hurting, or those with special needs. Show us how to be present in our neighborhood as you were present to us in the incarnation. Lead us through those you have called to leadership among us.

Establish your kingdom, O God.

The zeal of the Lord will accomplish it.

Everlasting Father, all people on earth bear your image. Provide for those who need food, clean water, shelter, education, or safety. Protect those who experience injustice of all kinds. The world is big and its needs are great. Therefore,

Establish your kingdom, O God.

The zeal of the Lord will accomplish it.

Prince of Peace, the nations are at war. There is conflict of many kinds—terrorism, prejudice, and fear. Would you come quickly to set all things right, for we long for the peace of your promise? We long for righteousness and justice to have the last word.

Establish your kingdom, O God.

The zeal of the Lord will accomplish it.

Amen.

December 31, 2017

Isaiah 60:10–62:3; Psalm 148; Galatians 4:4-7; Luke 2:22-40

Gathering Prayer

On this first Sunday after Jesus's birth, we remember all that is new: an infant in a manger, the presence of God with us, whispers of the purpose of this child's life, the very hope of salvation. What is new carries echoes of what has gone before. We remember how children always move the story of salvation forward—Isaac, Moses, and Obed to Ruth and Naomi. We remember the presence of God guiding the people through the wilderness. We remember the promises and the hope—ever ancient and ever new—that draw us to worship today.

Preaching Theme

Eugene Peterson has a book entitled *A Long Obedience in the Same Direction*—a good title for a sermon based on this Gospel text. If you are prone to dismiss religious practice as merely "going through the motions," know this: Simeon and Anna were not "accidentally" in the right place at the right time. They had trained themselves for this moment. They knew what they were looking for and recognized him when they saw him, although he would have been an infant quite like any other. Who looks in the drooly face of an infant and sees the wisdom of the ages? Who hears a baby's coos and conjures up a cross and crown of thorns, a grave and the redemption of Israel? Fred Craddock says, "These two aged saints are Israel in miniature, and Israel at its best: devout, obedient, constant in prayer, led by the Holy Spirit, at home in the temple, longing and hoping for the fulfillment of God's promises."[5] Simeon and Anna are seasoned and prepared by a lifetime's obedience in the same direction.

Secondary Preaching Themes

Luke's Gospel refers to "the law" nine times. Five of those nine times appear in our Gospel text. Mary and Joseph do everything "in keeping with what's stated in the Law of the Lord" (Luke 2:24). We ought never to forget that Jesus was raised Jewish.

In later life, he'll have some things to say about the abuses of the tradition, but we can never forget that he was speaking to his own. He wasn't an outsider raining down persecutions and judgments. Jesus was steeped in the law from earliest days, delighting in the covenant relationship it signified between God and the people of God.

Even Paul, who is no fan of the way things used to be, recognizes the necessity of a Messiah born under the law to redeem and fulfill that same law. Paul's argument is not that the children grow up to belong to someone else but, rather, that children grow into their belonging and into their inheritance through Christ and by the power of his Spirit at work.

If we are inclined to take the birth of Jesus as a radical discontinuity from the work of God in Israel, we need look no further than Isaiah for our corrective. The promise of fulfillment is the hope of the waiting people of God. As we long for Christ to come again and redeem all things, ours is a continuous hope for we, too, are the waiting people of God. Let us train and discipline ourselves, like Simeon and Anna, for a lifetime's obedience in the same direction.

Responsive Reading (Based on Psalm 148)

All: Praise the Lord!

LV: Praise the Lord from heaven! Praise God on the heights!

HV: Praise God, all of you who are his messengers. Praise God, all of you who comprise his heavenly forces!

LV: Sun and moon, praise God! All of you bright stars, praise God!

HV: You highest heaven, praise God! Do the same, you waters that are above the sky!

One: Let all of these praise the Lord's name because God gave the command and they were created! God set them in place always and forever. God made a law that will not be broken.

LV: Praise the Lord from the earth, you sea monsters and all you ocean depths!

HV: Do the same, fire and hail, snow and smoke, stormy wind that does what God says!

LV: Do the same, you mountains, every single hill, fruit trees, and every single cedar!

HV: Do the same, you animals—wild or tame—you creatures that creep along and you birds that fly!

LV: Do the same, you kings of the earth and every single person, you princes and every single ruler on earth!

HV: Do the same, you young men—young women too! You who are old together with you who are young!

One: Let all of these praise the Lord's name because only God's name is high over all. Only God's majesty is over earth and heaven. God raised the strength of his people, the praise of all his faithful ones—that's the Israelites, the people who are close to him.

All: Praise the Lord!

(LV: low voice; HV: high voice)

Benediction (Based on Luke 2:29-32)

Triune God—Father, Son, and Holy Spirit—you prepared this salvation in the presence of all peoples.

Our eyes have seen your salvation—a light of revelation, the glory of your people.

Holy God, let your servants go in peace according to your word.

Excerpt from *Preaching in Pictures: Using Images for Sermons That Connect*
by Peter Jonker

Peter Jonker wants to help preachers move from what he calls "the beautiful mess" of early sermon preparation to a unified and vibrant message that is propelled by a controlling image. In his book, Jonker suggests numerous sources for preachers to locate such imagery, and in this excerpt he commends especially an apprenticing of ourselves to the art of poets.

....

Who might help us hone our craft? The poets might help us. Preachers have used images over the years, but when it comes to choosing and molding a metaphor, we are rank amateurs compared to poets. Poets have been working with images from the beginning. As long as poetry has existed, men and women have been trying to find good metaphors for their compositions. As long as poetry has existed, men and women have been trying to understand how images work and where their power comes from. If we preachers want to write sermons that use controlling images effectively, we could learn a thing or two from the poets...

Poets and preachers face similar challenges. Like preachers, poets start with a beautiful mess, all of it collected from their textual observations. Of course their messes come from a different text. While preachers compile their messes from reading and studying a Bible passage, poets make their messes by examining the world around them. A poet's text is life and all its stuff: relationship dynamics, natural phenomena, personal feelings—the poet is constantly looking at all of these for inspiration. Every day as the poet reads the paper and mows the lawn and talks to colleagues and buys the groceries and takes children to piano lessons, the poet will observe a thousand remarkable things happening in the world. All of them may be interesting to the poet, but to make a poem he or she must somehow choose one bit of experience, one image, one incident from the beautiful mess and make it sing. Somehow one small portion of life, one small observation of the world is made to stand for more than itself. Or to put it in the words of poet Mary Oliver: "What is poetry but, through whatever particular instance seems to be occurring, a meditation on something more general and more profound."[1] So just like preachers, poets find one image in the beautiful mess and they use it to propel their work…

How do poets harness the image's power? They start with a blank sheet of paper and the sprawl of personal experience; out of this beautiful mess, how do they manage to pluck one perfect image around which to build a poem?

It's not easy. Poets are hunters, looking for a phrase, a picture, a newspaper headline, an evocative moment that will sprout into a poem. They prod the beautiful mess of their experiences, turning over rocks, combing the dark corners of their attics looking for something that will take hold of their imaginations.

Sometimes the search can be long. Just as preachers will tell you that the hardest part of preaching is moving from the beautiful mess of exegesis to the specificity and structure of a good sermon, so poets will tell you that plucking a meaningful image out of the mess of their experiences is really difficult. Both poets and preachers find a blank sheet of paper intimidating.

Poet David Citino admits to being intimidated. He thinks that grabbing something out of the beautiful mess of your experience is definitely the hardest part of writing a poem, much harder than all the other technical aspects.

> Line breaks, rhythms, exigencies of form. A sonnet? That's easy. Fourteen lines of iambic pentameter. It's when we try to talk about the creation, the willing into existence of something palpable and living where before we could detect only blank space, the white page or the blank screen, that we find ourselves with a severe case of aphasia, or at least a prolonged spell of hemming and hawing.[2]

Prolonged spells of hemming and hawing. What preacher can't identify with that? We may have lots of information in front of us, we may start with a pile of good exegesis but that doesn't make it easy. Just ask poets Ted Kooser and Steve Cox:

> You are bombarded every moment with sensations—the sight of a cereus blossom on your morning walk, the sound of a curve-billed thrasher's call nearby, the taste lingering from breakfast, the smell of a creosote brush, the touch of a warm sweater on your arms—so many sensations that you may feel overwhelmed. Again, where do you begin?[3]

Fortunately, poets do more than hem and haw in answer to this question. As they describe the process, finding and using that one perfect image seems to involve three steps: seeing, specifying, and going deep. Together these three steps describe a trajectory, a path; the poem and its imagery propel first the poet, then the reader, on a kind of journey. We can map that journey: a good image takes the reader on a journey that begins in delight and ends in wisdom.

The language of "delight to wisdom" comes from Robert Frost. He said that this was "the figure a poem makes," which was his attempt to describe the way a poem propels the reader.

It begins in delight and ends in wisdom. It begins in delight, it inclines to the impulse, it assumes direction with a first line laid down, it runs a course of lucky events, and ends in a clarification of life—not necessarily a great clarification such as the sects and cults are founded on, but in a momentary stay against confusion.[4]

Preachers would benefit from following a little behind the poets and watching to see how they make this journey from delight to wisdom, because this isn't so different from the figure a sermon makes. We, too, want to communicate wisdom. We want to offer our listeners a (hopefully more than momentary) stay against confusion. Our attempts to communicate a sermon theme are pretty close to Frost's desire to bring a "clarification of life," and we also want to do it in a way that delights.

Excerpt from *Actuality: Real Life Stories for Sermons That Matter* by Scott Hoezee

From childhood forward, we learn about life mostly through the avenue of stories and storytelling. Yet many preachers often present sermons that are devoid of individual stories even as the sermons themselves lack an overall narrative structure and allure. In Actuality *Scott Hoezee commends the art of storytelling for more vibrant sermons that have traction in real life, and in this excerpt he ponders especially creative writing's #1 rule: Show, Don't Tell.*

....

When experienced writers talk about showing versus telling, they are describing a writing practice that at once makes for more interesting reading and that at the same time conveys information in a manner that will stick with the reader for much longer. The author Ron Rozelle, for instance, points out that by the time you finish reading Harper Lee's Pulitzer Prize–winning novel *To Kill a Mockingbird,* one thing that you as a reader are convinced of as much as anything else is that this novel's hero, Atticus Finch, is the epitome of a good man. Atticus Finch is the embodiment of goodness. But as Rozelle notes, not once in the course of that entire novel do you ever encounter the line "Atticus was a good man." Harper Lee never once *told* her readers that Atticus was good. Instead, in scene after scene, Lee *showed* her readers this man's goodness in ways that are indelible.[1]

My favorite scene from both the novel and from the film version of *To Kill a Mockingbird* demonstrates this principle of "Show, Don't Tell" in ways that are properly instructive for preachers. It is also a fine example that good storytelling comes from the details that get included. In the story, Atticus Finch is an attorney who nobly defends the wrongly accused black man, Tom Robinson, against the charge of having molested and raped a white woman. Despite Atticus's having mounted a credible case to demonstrate Tom Robinson's innocence, the all-white jury finds Robinson guilty anyway. From the courtroom balcony Finch's children, Jem and Jean Louise (or "Scout"), had been watching the proceedings among a great crowd of black people who had come to see the trial but who were segregated from sitting on the lower level. After the guilty verdict is announced and the court begins to clear, Harper Lee wrote the following in the narrative voice of the daughter, Jean Louise/Scout:

Dimly, I saw Atticus pushing papers from the table into his briefcase. He snapped it shut, went to the court reporter and said something, nodded to Mr. Gilmer, and then went to Tom Robinson and whispered something to him. Atticus put his hand on Tom's shoulder as he whispered. Atticus took his coat off the back of his chair and pulled it over his shoulder. Then he left the courtroom, but not by his usual exit. He must have wanted to go home the short way, because he walked quickly down the middle aisle toward the south exit. I followed the top of his head as he made his way to the door. He did not look up.

Someone was punching me, but I was reluctant to take my eyes from the people below us, and from the image of Atticus's lonely walk down the aisle.

"Miss Jean Louise?"

I looked around. They were standing. All around us and in the balcony on the opposite wall, the Negroes were getting to their feet. Reverend Sykes's voice was as distant as Judge Taylor's:

"Miss Jean Louise, stand up. Your father's passin'."[2]

This scene shows us the goodness of Atticus Finch—and the respect it garnered for him among the downtrodden people whom he served—in a way vastly more memorable and more meaningful than had Lee written at any point in her novel "Atticus Finch was a good man." But of course, that is but one such scene throughout the novel that shows what goodness looks like in action even if the trait of goodness is never once singled out for theoretical consideration. As Rozelle points out, it would surely be much more expedient to write "Atticus Finch was a good man" as opposed to the scene just quoted that requires many more words and takes up considerably more space on a page. But it is precisely the level of detail and the grain of real life that is experienced in the longer scene that makes goodness vivid.

Preachers take note! A few well-chosen narrative details deliver the freight of what needs to be conveyed better than dozens of abstract words or descriptions ever could. Of course, a novel and a sermon are two very different kinds of writing, but the underlying principle here applies to preaching as well as to novel writing: people learn best not primarily when something is explained to them but when through the inclusion of detail and elements of everyday life people *recognize* in a narrative way truths that resonate with their experience.

If you know someone in real life similar to Atticus Finch, then when you talk about that person to someone else, you also will reach for stories, vignettes, and details that show this person's goodness in action. Indeed, if you were merely to say to someone, "My friend Jane Hogan is a good person," the average person would likely respond, "What do you mean by 'good'? How so?" The answer to such a logical question will inevitably lead to stories chockfull of real-world details that will flesh out Jane's goodness.

Sermons do not exist merely to tell stories, nor do they move along only the way a novel would proceed. But whenever sermons talk about scenarios of real life, just *telling* people that Scenario X exists in the world will never be as effective as *showing* one clear and detailed example of that scenario in action. And please notice: if your just mentioning Jane's "goodness" in the abstract would not be enough to satisfy a conversation partner on a Tuesday morning over coffee, then it will not be acceptable on a Sunday morning when talking about the goodness of God. When the preacher says "My Savior is a good person," those listening will respond in their hearts "What do you mean by 'good'? How so?"

Excerpt from *The Sermon without End: A Conversational Approach to Preaching*
by Ronald Allen and O. Wesley Allen Jr.

Authors Ronald Allen and O. Wesley Allen Jr. believe we are living in what they term a postapologetic age in which all communication—including sermons, therefore—perforce exist within a matrix of other conversations and other sources of authority that surround us. In this excerpt the authors ponder how the monologue of the sermon can encounter the meaning-making dialogues in which we engage every day.

Preachers who desire to foster and fund authentic postapologetic conversation shape their sermons

> to contribute to postmodern individuals' and communities' approaches to making meaning in a pluralistic setting by offering a tentative interpretation of, experience of, and response to God's character, purposes, and good news.

The postapologetic sermon *contributes to the meaning-making processes of those in the pews*. It does not define truth that is persuasive and, therefore, must be acknowledged and accepted by all. It does not name what all in the community must find meaningful and must believe and do, or must leave behind when they exit the building after the service. Preachers try instead to offer the sermon as a resource that postmodern hearers use to make meaning of God, the world, and their lives in conversation with the many other resources on which they draw day after day, week after week, year after year.

Serving as a resource instead of trying to name what must be believed in some authoritarian fashion does not mean that postapologetic preachers do not "proclaim" anything, that they just throw out provocative questions that get the congregation's juices flowing, or that they just offer a bulleted list of different possibilities and then sit down leaving the hearers to choose. The postapologetic sermon can and should unapologetically be a thoroughly Christian sermon, setting out particular claims about *God's character, purposes, and good news* through the lens of the Christ event as named and renamed in the church's scriptures, traditions, and practices.

Indeed, the preacher can and should *proclaim* such things . . . but does so humbly, in a tone open to commendation of and critique by other perspectives. The preacher offers the proclamation as of ultimate meaning for her or him without declaring it as absolutely meaningful and binding for all.

The postapologetic sermon takes this sort of stance by *offering a tentative interpretation of, experience of, and response to* God's character, purposes, and good news. The key word here is *tentative*. Fred Craddock has often said that a sermon cannot be called good news if there is no room for the listener to say no to it. Preachers commend something to the congregation; they do not dictate something for them. Their proclamation grows out of their particular situatedness and training. Hopefully, their social location, faith, and vocation lead them to be passionate about the kerygma that they proclaim, but such passion should not give way to an arrogant sense of absolute correctness. Postapologetic preachers proclaim provisionally as they represent Christian faith from the perspective of the congregation's tradition in their own individual voices:

- "This is what I believe the church believes, and that it is worthy of you considering believing."

- "This is my studied interpretation of the scriptures, traditions, and practices of the church that I offer to you."

- "This is *an* experience of the gospel I offer you to experience."

- "This is a response to God I value and commend to you. And after worship, I would welcome your reaction, critique, and your counter-commendation."

The humble commendation of a particular perspective of Christian faith in a postapologetic sermon maintains the same sort of ethics needed for authentic conversation. Even though structurally it is a monologue, the sermon is still "at heart a kind of social relation." . . . The preacher is both the facilitator of the conversation and the only one who speaks in it. This means that the preacher must be especially attentive to valuing reciprocity and asymmetry in and around the monological, conversational sermon. This means that preachers must view the congregation as a matrix of conversations in which this monologue participates.[1]

This reciprocal listening is a sign that the preacher values asymmetry in the congregation (and in the world in, and with, which the congregation interacts and makes meaning). But valuing it in terms of our own growth as a postmodern individual, or even in terms of the general shape of a postmodern congregation, is not enough. Preachers must value and represent some degree of asymmetry *in* their sermons. They must find ways to represent a diversity of serious voices found in and around the congregation in their sermons so that hearers can engage a range of perspectives in considering the tentative proposal being offered by the Preacher.[2]

In doing so, preachers must be careful to represent those voices in ways the others being represented would value, that is, in ways that, best as possible in a monologue, allow the others to name themselves and their positions. The call to bring other voices into the sermon, however, does not entail that postapologetic preachers should relinquish all authority in the pulpit. To do so would be as unethical as to claim unquestionable authority. Preachers have been ordained or commissioned by denominational judicatories and the congregation to represent their tradition.

They have been trained in and set aside by the church to continue studying the scriptures, traditions, and practices of the church on behalf of the church. Preachers are certainly authorized to offer informed, yet tentative interpretations of these scriptures, traditions, and practices. Indeed, congregations *need* them to do so. The preacher, however, has no more authority in the arenas of reason or experience than anyone else in worship. There are likely smarter persons in the pews than in the pulpit. There are congregants better trained in science, economics, political theory, sociology, humanities, and arts than the preacher. Similarly, the preacher has no better qualifications in the arena of experience than parishioners. Those in the pews have had different and varied experiences of the world and God-in-the-world than the preacher. They know joy and suffering, guilt and grace in a myriad of ways. They have traveled to places unvisited by the preacher and known a range of people the preacher has never met. The preacher has the authority and ethical responsibility to offer a tentative interpretation of, experience of, and response to God's character, purposes, and good news so that the hearers can bring the homiletical proposal into conversation with their own knowledge and experience as they construct meaning in and of the world.

Recommended Resources

Allen, O. Wesley, Jr. *Preaching and the Human Condition: Loving God, Self, and Others*. Nashville: Abingdon Press, 2016.

Allen, Ronald J. *Preaching: An Essential Guide*. Nashville: Abingdon Press, 2002.

————. *Sermon Treks: Trailways to Creative Preaching*. Nashville: Abingdon Press, 2013.

————. *Thinking Theologically: The Preacher as Theologian*. The Elements of Preaching Series. Minneapolis: Fortress Press, 2008.

Allen, Ronald J., and O. Wesley Allen Jr. *The Sermon Without End: A Conversational Approach to Preaching*. Nashville: Abingdon Press, 2015.

Armstrong, Jacob, with Adam Hamilton and Mike Slaughter. *The New Adapters: Shaping Ideas to Fit Your Congregation*. Nashville: Abingdon Press, 2015.

Bandy, Thomas G., with Lucinda Suzanne Holmes. *Worship Ways: For the People Within Your Reach*. Nashville: Abingdon Press, 2014.

Barnes, Craig. *The Pastor as Minor Poet: Texts and Subtexts in the Ministerial Life*. Grand Rapids, MI: Wm. B. Eerdmans, 2009.

Boers, Arthur. *Servants and Fools: A Biblical Theology of Leadership*. Nashville: Abingdon Press, 2015.

Calvin Theological Seminary. Center for Excellence in Preaching. cep.calvin seminary.edu.

Chakoian, Christine. *Cryptomnesia: How a Forgotten Memory Could Save the Church*. Nashville: Abingdon Press, 2014.

Cleaver, Emanuel, III. *Pastor on Track: Reclaiming Our True Role*. Nashville: Abingdon Press, 2014.

Craddock, Fred. *Craddock on the Craft of Preaching*. St. Louis: Chalice Press, 2013.

————. *Preaching*. 25th Anniversary ed. Nashville: Abingdon Press, 2010.

Davis, Josh and Nikki Lerner. *Worship Together in Your Church as in Heaven*. Nashville: Abingdon Press, 2015.

Farris, Patricia. *Five Faces of Ministry: Pastor, Parson, Healer, Prophets, Pilgrim*. Nashville: Abingdon Press, 2015.

Graves, Mike. *The Fully Alive Preacher: Recovering from Homiletical Burnout*. Louisville: Westminster John Knox, 2006.

Gutenson, Charles E. *Church Worth Getting Up For*. Nashville: Abingdon Press, 2013.

Hamilton, Adam. *Speaking Well: Essential Skills for Speakers, Leaders, and Preachers*. Nashville: Abingdon Press, 2015.

Hoezee, Scott. *Actuality: Real Life Stories for Sermons that Matter*. The Artistry of Preaching Series. Nashville: Abingdon Press, 2014.

Hogan, Lucy Lind. *Graceful Speech: An Invitation to Preaching*. Louisville: Westminster John Knox, 2006.

Jonker, Peter. *Preaching in Pictures: Using Images for Sermons That Connect*. The Artistry of Preaching Series. Nashville: Abingdon Press, 2015.

Kallas, Ellsworth. *Preaching in an Age of Distraction.* Downers Grove, IL: Inter Varsity Press, 2014.

LaRue, Cleophus James. *The Heart of Black Preaching.* Louisville: Westminster John Knox, 1999.

———. *I Believe I'll Testify: The Art of African American Preaching.* Louisville: Westminster John Knox, 2011.

Lischer, Richard. *The End of Words: The Language of Reconciliation in a Culture of Violence.* Grand Rapids, MI: Wm. B. Eerdmans, 2005.

Long, Thomas G. *Preaching and the Literary Forms of the Bible.* Minneapolis: Fortress Press, 1988.

———. *Testimony: Talking Ourselves into Being Christian.* San Francisco: Jossey-Bass, 2004.

———. *What Shall We Say? Evil, Suffering, and the Crisis of Faith.* Grand Rapids, MI: Wm. B. Eerdmans, 2014.

———. *The Witness of Preaching.* Rev. Ed. Louisville: Westminster John Knox, 2005.

Lose, David. *Preaching at the Crossroads: How the World—and Our Preaching—Is Changing.* Minneapolis: Fortress Press, 2013.

Lowry, Eugene L. *The Homiletical Beat: Why All Sermons Are Narrative.* Nashville: Abingdon Press, 2012.

———. *The Homiletical Plot: The Sermon as Narrative Art Form.* Louisville: Westminster John Knox, 2000.

McClure, John S. *Preaching Words: 144 Key Terms in Homiletics.* Louisville: Westminster John Knox, 2007.

Moss, Otis, III. *Blue Note Preaching in a Post-Soul World: Finding Hope in an Age of Despair.* Louisville: Westminster John Knox, 2015.

Pagitt, Doug. *Preaching in the Inventive Age.* Nashville: Abingdon Press, 2014.

Plantinga, Cornelius, Jr. *Reading for Preaching: The Preacher in Conversation with Storytellers, Biographers, Poets, and Journalists.* Grand Rapids, MI: Wm. B. Eerdmans, 2013.

Sweet, Leonard. *Giving Blood: A Fresh Paradigm for Preaching.* Grand Rapids, MI: Zondervan, 2014.

Taylor, Barbara Brown. *The Preaching Life.* Norwich: Canterbury Press, 2013.

The Text This Week: Lectionary, Scripture Study Worship Links, and Resources. www.textweek.com.

Thomas, Frank. *They Like to Never Quit Praisin' God: The Role of Celebration in Preaching.* Cleveland: The Pilgrim Press, 2013.

———. *Introduction to African American Preaching.* Nashville: Abingdon Press, 2016.

Tisdale, Nora Tubbs. *Prophetic Preaching: A Pastoral Approach.* Louisville: Westminster John Knox, 2010.

Troeger, Thomas H. *Sermon Sparks: 122 Ideas to Ignite Your Preaching.* Nashville: Abingdon Press, 2011.

———. *So That All Might Know: Preaching that Engages the Whole Congregation.* Nashville: Abingdon Press, 2008.

———. *Wonder Reborn: Creating Sermons on Hymns, Music, and Poetry.* Oxford: Oxford University Press, 2010.

Troeger, Thomas H., and Leonora Tubbs Tisdale. *A Sermon Workbook:*

Exercises in the Art and Craft of Preaching. Nashville: Abingdon Press, 2013.

Wallace, Robin Knowles. *The Christian Year: A Guide for Worship and Preaching.* Nashville: Abingdon Press, 2011.

Willimon, William. *How Odd of God: Chosen for the Curious Vocation of Preaching.* Louisville: Westminster John Knox, 2015.

———. *Pastor: The Theology and Practice of Ordained Ministry.* Rev. Ed. Nashville: Abingdon Press, 2016.

Wilson, Paul Scott. *The Four Pages of the Sermon: A Guide to Biblical Preaching.* Abingdon Press, 1999.

———. *The Practice of Preaching.* Rev. Ed. Nashville: Abingdon Press, 2007.

———. *Preaching as Poetry: Beauty Goodness, and Truth in Every Sermon.* The Artistry of Preaching Series. Nashville: Abingdon Press, 2014.

Working Preaching. www.workingpreacher.org.

Resources by the Contributors

Allen, Ronald J., and O. Wesley Allen Jr. *The Sermon Without End: A Conversational Approach to Preaching*. Nashville: Abingdon Press, 2015.

Allen, O. Wesley, Jr. *Preaching and the Human Condition: Loving God, Self, and Others*. Nashville: Abingdon Press, 2016.

Davis, Josh and Nikki Lerner. *Worship Together in Your Church as in Heaven*. Nashville: Abingdon Press, 2015.

del Rosario, DJ. *Wind in the Wilderness: A Lenten Study from the Prophets*. Nashville: Abingdon Press, 2016.

deVega, Magrey. *Awaiting the Already: An Advent Journey Through the Gospels*. Nashville: Abingdon Press, 2015.

deVega, Magrey, with Steve Harper. *Five Marks of a Methodist: Leaders Guide*. Nashville: Abingdon Press, 2016.

———. *Five Marks of a Methodist Participant Character Guide*. Nashville: Abingdon Press, 2016.

Foskett, Mary F., and O. Wesley Allen Jr. *Between Experience and Interpretation: Engaging the Writings of the New Testament*. Nashville: Abingdon Press, 2008.

Harper, Steve, and Magrey deVega. *Five Marks of a Methodist: DVD*. Nashville: Abingdon Press, 2016.

Hoezee, Scott. *Actuality: Real Life Stories for Sermons that Matter*. The Artistry of Preaching Series. Nashville: Abingdon Press, 2014.

Jonker, Peter. *Preaching in Pictures: Using Images for Sermons that Connect*. The Artistry of Preaching Series. Nashville: Abingdon Press, 2015.

Lewis, Karoline. *John*. Minneapolis: Fortress Press. 2014.

———. *She: Five Keys to Unlock the Power of Women in Ministry*. Nashville: Abingdon Press, 2016.

Smith, Ted. *The New Measures: A Theological History of Democratic Practice*. Cambridge: Cambridge University Press, 2012.

Willimon, William. *Bishop: The Art of Questioning Authority by an Authority in Question*. Nashville: Abingdon Press, 2012.

———. *Incarnation: The Surprising Overlap of Heaven and Earth*. The Belief Matters Series. Nashville: Abingdon Press, 2013.

———. *Pastor: The Theology and Practice of Ordained Ministry*. Rev. Ed. Nashville: Abingdon Press, 2016.

———. *Resident Aliens: Life in the Christian Colony*. 25th Anniversary Ed. Nashville: Abingdon Press, 2014.

———. *Thank God It's Friday: Encountering the Seven Last Words from the Cross*. Nashville: Abingdon Press, 2006.

———. *Thank God It's Thursday: Encountering Jesus at the Lord's Table as If for the Last Time*. Nashville: Abingdon Press, 2013.

———. *Why Jesus?* Nashville: Abingdon Press, 2010.

Wilson, Paul Scott. *The Four Pages of a Sermon*. Nashville: Abingdon Press, 1999.

————. *New Interpreters Handbook of Preaching.* Nashville: Abingdon Press, 2008.

————. *The Practice of Preaching.* Nashville: Abingdon Press, 2007.

————. *Preaching as Poetry: Beauty, Goodness, and Truth in Every Sermon.* Nashville: Abingdon Press, 2014.

Notes

January

1. Andy Stanley, *Deep and Wide: Creating Churches Unchurched People Love to Attend* (Grand Rapids: Zondervan, 2012), Kindle edition, locations 545–46.

2. Beverly Roberts Gaventa, *The New Interpreter's Bible One-Volume Commentary* (Nashville: Abingdon Press, 2010), Kindle edition, location 16372.

3. National Association for the Advancement of Colored People, "Separate and Unequal," http://action.naacp.org/page/-/images/press/Separate%20and%20Unequal.pdf.

4. National Association for the Advancement of Colored People, "Criminal Justice Fact Sheet," http://www.naacp.org/pages/criminal-justice-fact-sheet.

March

1. Alice Walker, *The Color Purple* (New York: Washington Square Press, 1978).

2. Ibid., 178.

3. Parker J. Palmer, *Let Your Life Speak: Listening to the Voice of Vocation* (San Francisco: Jossey-Bass, 2000).

4. Ibid., 44–46.

5. James Luther Mays, *Psalms* (Louisville: John Knox Press, 1994), 118.

April

1. John Irving, *A Prayer for Owen Meany* (New York: Ballantine Books, 1989), 111.

May

1. Quoted in Gerhard Ulhorn, *Christian Charity in the Ancient Church* (New York: Scribner and Sons, 1883), 153.

July

1. Eugene Peterson, *The Message: The New Testament in Contemporary Language* (Colorado Springs: Navpress, 1993), 31.

2. Dixie Chicks, vocal performance of "Cowboy Take Me Away," by Martie Seidel and Marcus Hummon, released in 1999 on *Fly*, compact disc.

3. Wendell Berry, *Given: Poems* (Berkley, CA: Counterpoint, 2005), 18.

4. Franz Kafka, "Before the Law," in *Parables and Paradoxes*, ed. Nahum N. Glatzer (Berlin: Schocken Books, 1961). The rendition herewith is adapted for the preacher's voice.

December

1. N. T. Wright, *For All God's Worth: True Worship and the Calling of the Church* (Grand Rapids, MI: Eerdmans, 1997), 1.

2. John Calvin, *Institutes of the Christian Religion* 2.15.2.

3. Phillips Brooks, "O Little Town of Bethlehem," *The United Methodist Hymnal* (Nashville: The United Methodist Publishing House, 1989), 230.

4. Isaac Watts, "Joy to the World," *The United Methodist Hymnal* (Nashville: The United Methodist Publishing House, 1989), 246.

5. Fred B. Craddock, *Luke*, Interpretation: A Bible Commentary for Teaching and Preaching (Louisville: Westminster John Knox, 2009), 40.

Preaching in Pictures Excerpt

1. Mary Oliver, *Rules for the Dance: A Handbook for Reading and Writing Metrical Verse* (Boston: Houghton Mifflin, 1998), 70.

2. David Citino, ed., *The Eye of the Poet: Six Views of the Art and Craft of Poetry* (New York: Oxford University Press, 2002), 178.

3. Ted Kooser and Steve Cox, *Writing Brave and Free* (Lincoln, NE: Bison Books, 2006), 21.

4. Robert Frost, "The Figure a Poem Makes," in *Modern Poetics*, ed. James Scully (New York: McGraw Hill, 1965), 56.

Actuality Excerpt

1. Ron Rozelle, "Balancing Description & Summary" in *Crafting Novels and Short Stories: The Complete Guide to Writing Great Fiction* (Blue Ash, OH: Writer's Digest Books, 2011), 238.

2. Harper Lee, *To Kill a Mockingbird* (New York: J. B. Lippincott Company, 1960), 214.

The Sermon without End Excerpt

1. See O. Wesley Allen Jr., *The Homiletic of All Believers: A Conversational Approach to Proclamation and Preaching* (Louisville: Westminster John Knox, 2005), 17–21.

2. For a model of representation of other voices in a collaborative homiletical model, see John S. McClure, *The Roundtable Pulpit: Where Leadership and Preaching Meet* (Nashville: Abingdon Press, 1995).

Contributors: Lectionary Sermon and Worship Helps

Sheila Bouie-Sledge—Pastor, Salem United Methodist Church, St. Louis, MO
February 26, 2017; March 5, 2017; March 12, 2017; March 19, 2017

....

Emanuel Cleaver III—Senior Pastor, St. James United Methodist Church, Kansas City, MO
January 29, 2017; February 5, 2017; February 12, 2017; February 19, 2017

....

Lora Copley—Christian Reformed Minister, Navajo Nation, Gallup, NM
December 10, 2017; December 17, 2017

....

Josh Davis—Multiethnic Worship Leader, founder of Proskuneo, Clarkston, GA
August 20, 2017; August 27, 2017; September 3, 2017; September 10, 2017

....

Yvette Davis—Pastor, Grace United Methodist Church, Harrisburg, PA
November 12, 2017; November 19, 2017; November 26, 2017; December 3, 2017

....

DJ del Rosario—Pastor, Bothell United Methodist Church, Bothell, WA
January 6, 2017; January 8, 2017; January 15, 2017; January 22, 2017

....

Magrey deVega—Pastor, Hyde Park United Methodist Church, Tampa, FL
September 17, 2017; September 24, 2017; October 1, 2017; October 8, 2017

....

Chelsey Harmon—Pastor, Christ Community Church, Nanaimo, BC, Canada
October 15, 2017; October 22, 2017; October 29, 2017; November 5, 2017

....

Scott Hoezee, General Editor—Director, The Center for Excellence in Preaching, Calvin
Theological Seminary, Grand Rapids, MI
July 30, 2017; August 6, 2017; August 13, 2017

Juan Huertas—Pastor, Grace Community United Methodist Church, Shreveport, LA
June 4, 2017; June 11, 2017; June 18, 2017; June 25, 2017

Meg Jenista—Pastor, The Washington DC Christian Reformed Church, Washington, DC
April 13, 2017; December 24, 2017; December 25, 2017; December 31, 2017

Gerald Liu—Assistant Professor of Homiletics and Worship, Drew University, Madison, NJ
March 26, 2017; April 2, 2017; April 9, 2017; April 14, 2017

Todd Maberry—Senior Director, Admissions, Recruitment, and Student Finance, Duke
Divinity School, Durham, NC
May 14, 2017; May 21, 2017; May 25, 2017; May 28, 2017

Erin Wathen—Pastor, Saint Andrew Christian Church, Olathe, KS
*April 16, 2017; April 23, 2017; April 30, 2017; May 7, 2017; July 2, 2017; July 9,
2017; July 16, 2017; July 23, 2017*

Contributors: Full Sermon Texts

O. Wesley Allen Jr.—Professor of Homiletics and Worship, Lexington Theological Seminary, Lexington, KY
"Jesus and Mosquito Bites" (Matthew 4:1-11)
"Outside the Door to the Christian Life" (Matthew 13:44-46)

Meg Jenista—Pastor, The Washington DC Christian Reformed Church, Washington, DC
"Like a Shepherd" (Psalm 23)

Karoline Lewis—Associate Professor of Biblical Preaching, Luther Seminary, St. Paul, MN
"Abundant Joy" (John 17:6-19)

Lia McIntosh—Community Opportunity Organizer, appointed by Missouri Conference, United Methodist Church, Kansas City, MO
"The Urgency of Now" (Micah 6:1-8)

Ted A. Smith—Associate Professor of Preaching and Ethics, Candler School of Theology, Atlanta, GA
"After Meeting Glory" (Exodus 24:12-18)

William Willimon—Professor of the Practice of Christian Ministry, Duke Divinity School, Durham, NC
"With Glad and Generous Hearts" (Acts 2:42-47)
"A Whisper, A Shout" (Matthew 10:26-27)

Index of Scripture

Visit cokesbury.com to download a free PDF of
The Abingdon Preaching Annual 2017. Password: A2C0P1A7